I Was Broken in All the Right Places

William McGee

ISBN 978-1-0980-9852-0 (paperback)
ISBN 979-8-88616-654-5 (hardcover)
ISBN 978-1-0980-9853-7 (digital)

Christian Faith Publishing
832 Park Avenue
Meadville, PA 16335
www.christianfaithpublishing.com

Printed in the United States of America

I give all glory to God, first for loving me when I didn't love myself enough, second for accepting me broken and transforming me to purpose, lastly for giving me the wisdom and courage to tell my story despite how ugly it might be. Thanks to my parents who have always been in my corner no matter how dark my life got at times. To my brother and sister who continued to believe in me. To my friends who stood in my corner, who saw both sides of my journey and never wavered in their friendship and love for me. To the Potters House Ministry and T. D. Jakes's obedience to speak the word and unadulterated truth. It was in many of the online messages I watch that led to the efforts of me writing this book. Last but of course not least, I dedicate this book to all those who will pick it up and read. I'm forever grateful for the opportunity to share my story with you all and for having the chance to speak into your life. My prayer for everyone is that your hearts be open and that you begin to allow God to heal, redeem, and transform your broken pieces into his intended purpose for your life.

INTRODUCTION

Let's be real—brokenness? It's not a sexy word or subject that most people want to discuss, especially when it comes to self-reflection. Our society is mostly filled with ways to cover up our cracks and deficiencies rather than empowering us to search them out, to understand the nature of how our broken pieces can be made to serve in the destiny of our purpose. I write this book not to condemn or judge who we've been or who we've become but to shed light and give hope to who God called us to be despite what our brokenness tells us we are. We are all broken to some degree; no one can escape it; there is no one perfect person outside of Christ. The good thing is God knows this about us all and accepts us as such. God doesn't call us to perfection but to progression toward our transformation into who he has called us to be. Discovering our internal brokenness is a part of our journey to become less of what the world calls acceptable and more of what God declared redeemable—meaning, God loved us even before he knew we'd be broken. When the Scripture tells us that we must carry our cross, it's because every day we must put ourselves on it. With this book and God's grace, I have the opportunity to put my life on the cross as a reflection of God's eternal glory and love for us. I share the story of my brokenness to convey that no matter how dark or ugly your past or life currently is, it's not wasted; there lies purpose among the pieces. The real question is, how deep and honest are you ready to get about who you've become and what you've done? I'll show my broken pieces; will you show us yours?

CONTENTS

PART 1

Trauma

"A psychological, emotional response to an event or an experience that is deeply distressing or disturbing that overwhelms an individual's ability to cope, causes feelings of helplessness, diminishes their sense of self and their ability to feel the full range of emotions and experiences. Trauma is defined by the experience of the survivor."

CHAPTER 1

Childhood

> Sometimes people can hunger for more than bread. It is
> possible that our children, our husband, our wife do not hunger
> for bread, do not need clothes, do not lack a house. But are
> we equally sure that none of them feels alone, abandoned,
> neglected, needing some affection? That, too, is poverty.
>
> —Mother Teresa

My soul began to die in the same place I was born. The day was March 10, 1986. As a child, I didn't understand what was happening. I was connected to the moment nonetheless. This could be said about trauma as well—I didn't recognize trauma as a child, only able to feel its affects. The power of trauma can influence and shape the fabric of who we become—it did for me. This is my story, where it all starts. I was raised in trauma.

Roots

Prior to March 10, 1986, my mother was involved in a gruesome car collision that nearly took her life. I didn't know what happened. As a child, I could only observe my mother struggling to move around the house, following her extensive surgery. My mom was in no condition to interact with me or my older brother at that time. Mom spent most days and nights in bed resting and healing, which put more responsibility on my father during her recovery. This made my father's plate full, attending to my mom's helpless agony, taking care of us boys while still providing for the household—a job truly fit for a real father.

My father was very meticulous about morning routines back then and still is to this day. On most early mornings during this time, my father prepared for the day holding to routine: he checked on my brother and I, attended to my mom, shaved and showered, and then went straight to the kitchen for the usual cup of morning coffee. With my mom on bed rest, my brother and I would cling to our father's every move, like most children. As my father enjoyed his routine cup of coffee, I looked on with curiosity and intrigue. I wasn't aware of what he was drinking then or any other important details, such as flavor, aroma, and most importantly, temperature. Like most inquisitive children, I took in the actions of the people that made up my environment. Those observations slowly began shaping my decision making.

I started walking early when I was a child, so I'd often be able to stand myself up using the coffee table for support. I practiced this often, trying to reach for that cup in anticipation to experience what I saw my father doing every morning with jubilation.

This morning was no different—I had propped myself up using the coffee table again, reaching ever intently for that cup. My father was not blind toward my intentions and aspirations; he watched me do this before. My father moved the cup out my reach like he did most mornings. At least that was his aim.

Unfortunately, it didn't pan out that way. My father didn't move it far enough out my reach like he'd intended, and with his attention turned away, I took my opportunity. I reached out my hand like I did most mornings. But this time, it was different. I had taken hold of the cup that stole my attention every morning. As I grabbed the cup, I begin emulating what I'd seen my father do so many times.

4

I took the cup, intending to drink it, but it didn't happen the way I had observed my father each and every morning. The weight of the cup made it impossible for me to bring to my lips. As I tilted the cup in eagerness, I missed my mouth completely, instead pouring the black liquid hot coffee all over my neck, chest, and stomach, burning me instantaneously.

As I begin to cry out in my unbearable and profound pain, my helpless and bedridden mother could only sit and listen to my distressed, pain-filled screams. My father ran toward me frantically in aid, not realizing until he got there that my screams where a result of his oversight.

My father picked me up and carried me off to my mother, rushing away to get cold towels to wrap me in, as the layers of skin begin to peel off my body. My mother neurotically swaddled me in cloth and had my father rush me immediately out of the house to the emergency room. Luckily we lived in close proximity to the hospital then.

Once my father and I arrived at the emergency room, the hospital admitted me to the ICU burn ward for immediate treatment, given the severity of my burns and my screams that echoed throughout the corridors.

The hospital would become my isolated prison. At least to me, that's what it would feel like, not having the capacity to rationalize my reality. I ended up staying in the hospital for several long dreadful weeks to heal from my wounds, petrified and having absolutely no clue where I was or why I was there. What made it more traumatizing for me was my parents were unable to stay with me overnight. Back then, the hospital had strict visiting policies and would only allow my parents to visit me during certain hours on specified days.

My parents had left me where I was once born, but this place was never meant to be my home. My father would visit when he was able to for those few weeks I was in there. My mother was never able to visit, given her own injuries from the accident and surgery.

I was in trauma but never knew it, trauma that hit me on every level. Mentally I had to observe the fact that I was all alone every day and didn't understand why, physically endured pain and discomfort from the burns, and the emotional toll of detachment from my family left me feeling abandoned.

Take a minute to think of the pages written in my life during those few weeks. The sense of abandonment grew in my spirit. The ramifications of this incident caused something in my soul to be broken. The hardest part of it all was that my birthday was March 19, only a week after I was severely burned. I'd celebrate a year of my life isolated, alone, abandoned, lost, scarred, frightened, and angry at the circumstance I was in, not surrounded by friends and family but alone in a hospital. This was my introduction to the world. This was the reality of my early childhood, the beginning stages of my life, the opening chapter of my ledger. This was a moment that unknowingly would impact the man I would become later on in life.

Symptoms

Growing up, my parents where both career-focused people, working hard to provide for my siblings and me. My father was an executive at a company that designed, manufactured, and sold airplanes, while my mother worked at a company that sold print and digital documents and services around the globe. My parents were both highly successful in their careers.

For me and my brother, this meant that during the day while my parents where away at work, we'd be in day care. Assimilating to childcare is easier for some than others—my transition into day care wasn't smooth at all. In fact, I dreaded entering that place every day.

I was fine on the car ride to the day care center. My parents would spend every morning reassuring and explaining to me why I was going to day care and that they would be gone for a few hours to work and come back to pick me up. I understood what my parents were saying but didn't understand what it meant. Children often see things as they are, not as they're meant to be, so was the case for me.

My parents did this every morning before dropping my brother and me off. It seemed to calm my nervousness up until the point we arrived. Then every time my parents would drop me off and begin to walk away, I would burst out screaming at the top of my lungs, begging for my parents not to leave me, begging to go with them, kicking and screaming to get out of day care.

Little did my parents know at that time, but this situation was all too familiar for me. For me, my parents weren't just dropping me off at day care—this scene reflected what had been written in my ledger. I'd feel the effects of this play out before. I remembered this story line and the behind-the-scenes trauma that came with it.

In my mind, I was back to being left and abandoned each day. Instead of a hospital, now it was a day care. I was reliving the beginning pages of my childhood. I was back in that hospital bed, lying in the dark, left all alone, only to watch the ones I knew and loved walk away once more. Even more, I don't know if anyone could hear behind my screams. Understand that it wasn't me screaming, it was my trauma. I didn't like to be left alone, feeling abandoned. Unfortunately, as a child, I was unable to reason that my childhood hospitalization debilitated my cognitive understanding of separation.

My parents saw this play out other times as well. Later on, around the ages of four and five, my attachment issues to my parents began to grow. Whenever not in the same room with them, I'd still need to be able to see my parents in my purview somehow out of fear of being left alone and abandoned. My inability to detach myself as a child fueled my fear of abandonment growing up. In parallel, this also quietly fueled anger from within, the anger that would spark later on in life. Even if my parents would go into another room and close the door, I would often be screaming and kicking profusely, often in fear, believing that I had been left again.

As I would grow up and leave behind my childhood, I assumed so would the thoughts and feelings of that trauma be left there as well. The truth though is that it never left me at all—maybe the symptoms of kicking and screaming and reacting as a child, sure; but the thought and fear of being abandoned and the root that was formed back in March of 1986 never died. It only manifested itself in other forms of my life, and I never dealt with the root, only always trimming at the symptoms of my trauma.

Drowning

I was young when it happened. We stayed at these townhomes at the time, which had a community pool that the residences would all enjoy mostly during the spring and summer seasons. It was about 5:00 or 6:00 p.m., close to dinner time. My parents sent me down to the pool to grab my older brother who had been swimming down at the pool all day with some friends. It was nice that day, and the pool was fairly packed.

I remember yelling to get my brother's attention as I stood by the poolside, but he didn't hear me as he kept going underneath the water to swim, plus it was quite loud with all the other kids running around, jumping in and out of the water. As I edged my way closer to the pool, continuing to shout to get my brothers attention, I somehow lost my footing and fell right in. I can still remember the feeling as I fell in, the instant fear and anxiety that came to mind, and the terrifying emotion as I begin to drown.

At the time, I didn't know how to swim—I had nothing to cling too, not my own abilities or even hope that someone saw me fall or noticed my struggle to come get me. I can recall the flashes of being in that hospital as a child again, yelling and screaming as my cries for help fell on deaf ears. I was scared and all alone now, I felt abandoned once more. I needed a miracle.

My miracle came when another kid happened to see me fall in and jumped into the water and saved me. To say I was traumatized when I came out of water would be an understatement—I was petrified. I remember my brother and other kids quickly coming over to check on me and console me, but all I could do was cry. This brush with mortality only compounded my feelings of abandonment, beginning the processes of drowning the depths of my soul in a pool of trauma.

Pages

Most researchers define the most important stages of a child's development are anywhere between the ages of one to seven. These can be the most crucial times children begin learning pertinent details about themselves and their environments. Walt Disney put it this way: "I think of a child's mind as a blank book. During the first years of his life, much will be written on the pages. The quality of that writing will affect his life profoundly."

I often didn't realize how the beginning pages I wrote in my ledger as a child contributed to traits in my character today. Often if we look at them, we'll see the roots of our becoming and maybe even the gestation of our shortcomings and brokenness. We might look back and say to ourselves, where did I go off track? How did I become like this? What have I forgotten in the ages, stages, and pages of my life that are affecting me today? How do I begin to address the early pages of my life so I can rewrite my story?

In order for me to answer those questions for myself, I had to begin to unravel the pages of my own trauma, my own pain and sufferings. I had to understand my trauma to better understand my story.

Sadly as a child, I was unable to confront my childhood experiences to understand who I was or what I was becoming. The growing pains never healed; they were only covered by age, continuing to live on in each stage of my life and writing my pages for me.

The Broken Piece: Abandonment

"Sometimes people can hunger for more than bread. It is possible that our children, our husband, our wife, do not hunger for bread, do not need clothes, do not lack a house. But are we equally sure that none of them feels alone, abandoned, neglected, needing some affection? That, too, is poverty," Mother Teresa so wisely said. Have you ever felt poor in this area? Have you ever felt undesired, discarded, or left behind? I can answer that with a resounding yes!

This is what I experienced, what sent me on a collision course of struggling with lifelong abandonment issues, never realizing the core issue. Spending those few weeks at the hospital in isolation, though a short time, left a deep and severe impact. Abandonment is "the act of intentionally and permanently giving up, surrendering, deserting, or relinquishing property, premises, a right of way, a ship, contract rights, a spouse and/or child." Don't confuse neglect with abandonment. Though they carry some similarities, they are distinctively two entirely different meanings. A simple way to contrast the two is that neglect is to withhold a good or service to others in our care, which impacts their well-being, while abandonment is to discard or desert entirely. Though neglect is often the first step toward abandonment.

For me, this started in the first few years of my life. I didn't know it then, because I didn't see the silent roots growing in me as a child. The memory and the pain that comes along with my experiences were forgotten, disregarded, and buried as I grew into adolescence and adulthood. I've seen the effects from leaving these issues untreated though, spreading across the pages of my life.

Among the many symptoms, I experienced an inability to commit to relationships, fear of intimacy, low self-esteem, mood swings and misplaced anger, an inability to be myself, a pessimistic perspective, the inability to trust others around me, appearing detached and closed off toward others. I often tried mending these indicators that came up in my life rather than the origin of my pain. It's often why I face difficulty with changing my habits because I hadn't confronted my past. I had to begin to understand my history if I was ever going to find my way to my destiny.

The abandonment I endured would be the hidden architecture that would shape my life. I never understood the moment; I only experienced the affects. Sometimes seeds get planted in our lives we never authorized. If we're not aware, we'll harvest fruit we never recognize from a tree that was never purified. This was my curse, or perhaps was simply a part of my purpose.

It would be years before I would be able to unpack that question. But one thing is clear, the root of trauma would set in motion a path and journey of broken pieces spread across multiple seasons of my life. You have read merely the beginning stage of my life. But over the next thirteen chapters, you'll read how the progression of my experiences lend to the cracks of my brokenness. Years later after my childhood, I would experience more trauma. Little did I know that it would come from the ones that I love the most, family.

CHAPTER 2

Family

To forgive is to set a prisoner free and
discover that the prisoner was you.

—Lewis B. Swedes

I didn't have a say; my family was chosen for me. This was my family, it's what I was raised in. We may not have a say in who we come from or our family members or the circumstance surrounding our childhood, but we do get to decide who we want to become once we're set free.

Characters

I believe family is the initial gateway to providence. But I didn't know the path to get there would be crooked or sometimes even broken. Between the ages of seven and sixteen, I was surrounded by a host of different characters within my family, all with diverse personalities, personas, biases, issues, values, attitudes, and perspectives. This is who God gave me, I never had a say in the matter.

My mother was a spitfire and social butterfly. Much of that hasn't changed. My mom has been a God-fearing woman for as long as I can remember, believing that having a true walk with God, consuming scripture and prayer, could solve all life's problems. To this day, my mother still has an infectious smile and personality. My mom has always been one to tell the truth and say it like it is, never one for sugarcoating her words or mincing points. My mother is as stern and straightforward as she is loving and nurturing, always wanting the best for me and our family. My father, however, was the complete opposite of my mother. Those two are like night and day, water and vinegar, one could postulate. My father has always been the more laid-back type, quiet and reserved, only speaks when he has something to say, not a man to show or express emotion. My father has a military background and has always had a consistent drive and advocacy for hard work and education, never believed in taking shortcuts in life. My father has always pushed us kids to give our best in anything we tackle and to never give up no matter how hard life gets. My parents have always strived to provide the best for us kids growing up. My parents would say, "We put needs before wants." But every once in a while, we got surprised with our wish list. I was close to my parents in my early years as described in the prior chapter, but that changed as I got older. In fact a lot would, but I'll get into that later.

During my early years, my closest relationship was my older brother, CJ, someone I looked up to and desired to be like when I was a child. Looking back now, I'd say I saw my brother as my protector. As a child, I knew CJ would always be there for me. CJ wasn't the perfect brother, but he's my brother nonetheless. My little sister, Terrika, soon arrived on the scene when I was eight years old. I love my brother and sister very much still to this day. But at times, growing up, I felt set apart. It can be unsettling sometimes to realize the ones we should be the closest to are the very ones we feel the farthest from. This was the case for me and my siblings as I got older.

My other relationships within my family were more intrinsically fragmented to some degree. For instance, my aunt Shannon, who often came around, was a model and college graduate. My aunt

Shannon's personality all alone would fill up a room in a moment's notice. She never had a problem showcasing her success, education, appearance, and flamboyancy whenever in attendance. I wouldn't use the words self-centered or stuck up to describe my aunt Shannon because I don't believe those were her intentions. But if people didn't know my aunt back then, individuals might consider adopting such nomenclatures. Aunt Shannon has always had very strong personality and an unwavering opinion about almost anything. I never really did have a close relationship with my aunt in my early years. I found it hard to truly ever see her and therefore connect with her. When I say "see," I don't mean in the physical since either. I mean see my aunt passed all those other elements like success, appearance, and education that looked almost to define her.

My uncle Chucky was a jokester and heavy alcoholic. I never saw the forty-ounce can Uncle Chucky would guzzle, only the ruffled brown paper bag that he held it in. Nonetheless my uncle Chucky was lighthearted and comical to be around. I enjoyed hanging out with my uncle. He had a way of creating laughter at a moment's notice. I took caution though, knowing my mother didn't always approve of me getting exposed to certain interactions when it came to my uncle Chucky. My uncle Charlie is a totally different story. He is as pleasant as he is vehemently violent. A real Dr. Jekyll and Mr. Hyde complex if there ever was one. The nickname that one of my cousins soon gave Uncle Charlie was Lucifer. Unfortunately the moniker still rings true to this day. The mere presence of Uncle Charlie would send most people into utter discomfort, fear, and sometimes even to different parts of the house that he wasn't in. My uncle Charlie has always had a long history of violence, abuse, and other questionable misconducts and allegations. I never feared my uncle Charlie. I was actually intrigued at the way others venerated him. But at young age, I didn't distinguish the reality that it was more disgust and fear than respect and admiration people had for him.

My aunt Diane, which I didn't spend much time with growing up, was medically declared schizophrenic when I was young. So I only saw my aunt on a handful of occasions. She's been institutionalized most of my life. My experiences with her were often short yet eventful. On one occasion, my mother and Aunt Diane got into a heated confrontation while at my grandma's house. The argument intensified to the point my aunt Diane snapped and started chasing my mother around the house with a kitchen knife, threatening to kill her. Luckily my dad showed up in the nick of time to wrestle the knife away and calm my aunt down. I saw my aunt again once after that, it was a better experience than the one I had previously. But as a child, I didn't know that my aunt was mentally ill at the time, so I was always somewhat nervous around her during my early years.

My great-aunt Birdell was as honest as she was loving. She was like big mama to most of our family. My mom loved my aunt and had a lot of similar traits to her as well. My aunt Birdell always said what needed to be heard, even if we didn't want to hear it. I'm sure some of us have a relative or two that's straightlaced that way. During family squabbles or arguments, I loved how my aunt never took sides but consistently pushed for peaceful outcomes instead. She's no longer with us, but I sure do miss my aunt's aura and the weight her voice carried in my family. There was a peace and stillness that came with my aunt Birdell. I could always find comfort in her words and much more in her presence. My grandma was always around. She preferred for people to call her Baby instead of grandma since she was the youngest out of her tribe. Grandma Baby was very easy going and loving. I always looked forward to my birthdays because Grandma would always have a nice envelope of cash for me and a big smile. Sadly my grandma Baby passed away while I was writing this book, but I was thankful for the moments I was able to share with her. I'll always miss how grandma baby would say my name. It had a southern draw to it that always brought me comfort. I spent most days after school at Grandma Baby's house and even whole summers there while my parents were away at work. It was a lot better than being in day care, that's for sure. It was at Grandma Baby's house where my siblings and I would spend time with all the family characters.

I was constantly around family during my early childhood and adolescent years. There was always a dinner gathering, celebration, or family festivity going on at someone's house. On most weekends, my parents hosted small house parties or social gatherings at the house to eat dinner, have drinks, and socialize with family and friends. It was during these times when I would see all the characters of my family members come to life, and they sure didn't disappoint. Almost every family gathering that I can recall turned into some form of violent altercation or verbal assault between individuals. I even had it out with my uncle Charlie on one of these occasions. The parties would always start on a good foot. But sometimes liquor mixed with family can alter that outcome quickly. My family members are all very loud and vociferous individuals with a lot of pride and ego to boot, each one of them carrying a very strong personality with them.

On one of these family occasions, my mom decided to throw a "welcome home" celebration for Uncle Chucky who had just gotten home from the military. At the time, my mom wasn't on good terms with Uncle Charlie and asked him not to come for the celebration. Uncle Charlie is my mom's brother as is Uncle Chucky. So my mom wasn't too happy when Uncle Charlie came strolling through the door for the celebration. My mom tried ignoring the situation as best she could but decided to confront my uncle Charlie in the kitchen before the festivities took off. That's just how my mom has always been, never one to hold her tongue. As always, the conversation started off normal, then grew with intensity as was the case with most arguments that went on at family get-togethers. The shouting from my uncle Charlie got so loud that my father had to warn him to back down and stop yelling and cursing so much at my mom, which only spawned an irrevocable reaction from Uncle Charlie. As the fight continued to get out of hand, Uncle Charlie did as well, so much so that he went to go strike my mom but was blocked by my father who ended up stabbing Uncle Charlie with a knife in the midst of the struggle. Frantic, Grandma Baby rushed Charlie to the hospital while the rest of my family continued to celebrate with Uncle Chucky and others. These violent outburst and occurrences didn't happen on a regular, but when they did, it only added to the continuation of more family drama. For me, these experiences where shocking, illuminating, and disruptive at a young age to see, but I didn't have a choice. This was my family.

It wasn't all bad though. I had many memorable moments with my family—the mini-weekend vacations to the ocean, the random road trips with mom's famous chicken and biscuits, the family barbecues, and many more other fun and exciting times. However the mix of these characters, no doubt, played a role in the values and moralities that I would draw on. Sometimes the characters surrounding our lives make up the characteristics in our lives if we're not careful. In my family, I saw and was exposed to pride and egos, alcoholics and drug dealers, pimps and players, mental illnesses and abusers, violence and anger, godly values and two parents striving hard to raise us kids in a loving household.

Lineage

It's fair to deduce that just about all of us could say that our families have impacted who we've become today. Whether that is for good or bad is largely up to each individual to determine. But family can be the first stage of insight into what some would say is our conceivable future. After all, for the first few years, it's all we come to know as a child—that is, until our innocence is abandoned or hijacked by the settle natures of our realities around us, which begin to set the tone for the man or woman we decide to become. Families, good or bad, have a catastrophic unknowingly huge responsibility of setting the course of our destiny. Even when I look back now, I can see how some of the turns and paths I chose to go down were in direct proportionate response to a family trauma, triumph, tradition, or tragedy. In those, we find the becoming of our character creation and the beginning courses of both our sufferings and celebrations. We must be cognizant of the branches that begin to take shape from the roots of our family trees, for it can come to bear fruit that nourishes or destroys us. Essentially our families are the first formation of sequences in our lives that have the potency to produce both life or death.

Though I love my family very much, it was one I felt disconnected from most of my life for many reasons. It's strange to consider how I could be disconnected to the very people I'm connected by. What does family mean when we feel set apart? How does the intricate laces of our family's history influence our stories? I once heard it said: "You can't spell *families* without *lies*." I never thought it would be talking about mine.

Whispers

Desmond Tutu, the prominent South African theologian and human rights activist, once said, "You don't choose your family. They are God's gift to you as you are to them." I'm sure a lot of us wish we could pick the family we come from, given our circumstances. But that just isn't the case. The hidden message behind that quote, I believe, is that some gifts don't always look shiny and brand-new. Some gifts, we have to work out. Bishop T. D. Jakes puts it this way: "Family is the gymnasium God gives us to work out our love in."

A gymnasium would be a great description for my household because there was a lot to work out, that's for sure. Of course I've seen a lot of fights and disputes with my extended family during gatherings and celebrations, but growing up in my household with my immediate family was no picnic all the time either.

As I said earlier, my parents where complete opposites, like dryland mixed with water. My mom has always had a very outspoken and sharp tongue. I say that with love and, of course, respect. But my mom has no problem voicing her concerns or issues. To this day, my siblings and I joke about this with our mom all the time. It's just how my mom is, and it isn't changing anytime soon. It's actually what I love the most about my mom though, because I know whatever problem I bring to her, my mother will always give me an honest opinion, not just one that benefits me. My father is not outspoken at all. When my mom gets loud, Pops gets quiet. My father has always been that way though, never one to argue, throw tempers, yell, or scream. He's just always been very calm and collected.

If there was one thing that my parents fought about the most, it would be about gambling. To this day, it's still kind of a sore subject in the household for all the pain, agony, and stress it has caused on my family. My father gambled a lot. It was his outlet—that and golf. But the gambling was something my father spent a lot of time doing and a lot of money on, something that never sit well with my mom at all. It caused a lot of problems under one roof. There would be many nights my father wouldn't even make it home after work because he'd spend the night gambling at the casino. We'd typically know when Pops got home though, because it was usually after everyone was asleep. My father would sneak in and sleep on the couch, but my mother knew when he'd get in and let him know how she felt. My mom wasn't quiet about it either. I used to wonder if my whole neighborhood knew our family drama, given how loud my mom could be. The gambling and the arguing always bothered my brother. And as I got older to understand what was going on, it started bothering me as well. I sometimes wonder if that's where my brother began to lose respect for our father and challenge him in ways that I dare wouldn't as a kid.

Nonetheless the gambling was an ongoing issue, a hard issue at that because my father was the breadwinner of the household and always said that as long as the bills were paid, the refrigerator was full, and we kids were okay, then there was nothing wrong with spending a few extra dollars on whatever he saw fit. It didn't get really bad until the gambling started effecting our livelihood. We almost lost our house on one or two occasions because of my father's gambling habits. It was a scary time for me. My parents were constantly at each other's throats and threatening each other with divorce, while my brother was seemingly getting into more and more trouble in school and with my parents. It's where the whispers would begin. It's where the story of my trauma would continue.

By the time I'd reach middle school, my home was a place I didn't want to be at. It was like a warzone, so bad I didn't even want to come out my room sometimes because there was always so much fighting, either with my mom and dad or my parents and my brother. My brother would always comfort me and tell me not to worry and that he'd always take care of me if anything was to happen with our parents, but my brother would also tell me something else, something that everyone else had been keeping a secret, something that caused a moment for me that would begin to alter my life completely—all with a few whispers.

Blindsided

My brother began rebelling often against my parents during my early teenage years, whether it be not listening and completely disobeying orders or disrespecting them blatantly in their face. It was clear, my brother didn't have a lot of respect for my parents growing up. Often when CJ and I would get in trouble, CJ would whisper little ideas in my head that I never fully understood. My brother would say things like "We don't have to listen to them, they're not really our parents," or "Our father is not really our father, we don't have to call him dad." I'd often just ignore it and go on about my business.

One of the most alarming moments in my household was the time my brother came home after being out all night after a school event. My parents hadn't heard from my brother nor did anyone else when my parents called around looking for him. It was sometime around the morning. My parents looked out the upstairs window from the dining room and saw my brother walking down the street. It was just him walking down the middle of the road. My parents, seemingly agitated and upset that my brother had been gone all night, raced to the door and began questioning where he had been and why he didn't come home or call. My brother didn't say a word, but tears were running down his face. My brother came into the house, walked directly into his bedroom, pulled out a handgun that apparently no one knew he even had, and began to walk back outside, clearly on a mission. My parents were able to plead with my brother in the front lawn of our house to give them the gun and come back inside. I felt the emotion from that day writing these words as I watched it happen from the stairway of our home. It wasn't uncommon in my household around this period of time. There was always something going on with my brother.

As we got older, my brother would show out and get in trouble even more and more with my parents and at times even curse back at our dad, saying, "I don't have to listen, we're not your kids." Again I would hear these comments but never understand why my brother would say it or what he meant by it. Once I confronted my mother about it after yet another skirmish had transpired between my parents and my brother. My mother at the time comforted me and told me, "Don't listen to your brother, he's just upset and acting out." So I did as my mom said and didn't worry about it anymore.

A year or two later, I'd soon come to the realization that everything I knew about our family wasn't all true. I'd soon come to understand why I felt set apart, why I felt disconnected to what I was connected by. Furthermore, it would shatter my identity of who I thought I was. It would soon become clear that all those little whispers that my brother would tell me about our parents not really being our family where actually somewhat true. Looking back on it now, I wonder if I would have decided to never have known the truth. See, up to that point, my family, though crazy at times, was all I had. How could the reality that my mother possibly lied to me be true?

Around the summertime, I was sitting downstairs in the living room of our family home when my mom came trickling down the stairs. In my mom's hand was a vanilla-stuffed envelope. I still have that envelope to this day. It was clear to me that my mom had something important to show me. I could tell because of the unsettledness of my mother's resolve. As my mom began to tell me the truth about my real father, the whispers of my brother's voice flowed through my inner ear and hovered over my heart with heaviness. It was hard for me to come to the realization that the man I knew my entire life, the man I came to love, respect, and honor, wasn't the man I thought he was. For me, I didn't know what hurt more, the lies, the new reality I found myself in, or the fact that my family wasn't really my family. As my mother continued to share the story about my biological father and the man I now call dad, I became angry and lost. I felt cheated, betrayed, misled, and put in a position I wasn't fit to withstand. As my mom began to share with me the content of what was inside the envelope, it became overwhelming for me to realize there was a whole other family out there that I came from. It was the first time I would see pictures of my father and other relatives I now had to comprehend as my family as well.

After telling me everything, my mom gave me some space to think and unwrap my thoughts, having just divulged what I could imagine was just as painful to share as it was for me to hear. There I sat looking through all the photos in the envelope, trying to put together the pieces of what this all meant, how the new idea of this other family would impact the relationship of my now current family. It didn't hit me until I saw the picture. There, beneath all the other photos of what I could only assume where cousins, aunts and uncles, and other family members, was a picture of my biological father. A picture of my father lying dead in an open casket. I don't know what I felt at the time, but I burst into tears. My heart was torn into pieces, and I didn't know why. So many thoughts came to my mind and heart all at once as I began to reason with who this man was and what could have been. I remember having so much rage in me, I hardly could keep myself together. Again something else broke in me, a new trauma. Sometimes the blinding disruptions in our life aren't meant to deter us but to mature us. But I wasn't ready for this disruption. I never got the chance to meet the man that was supposed to be my father. But again it added to my feeling of abandonment. But this broken piece was a different, one of anger and bitterness. My real father was found dead hanging from a tree. I don't know how or why, but it was the last fact of what I knew about a man that supposed to be my father, my family.

That moment, in the living room, took whatever innocence was left in me and threw it away. My stepfather soon came downstairs to comfort me and said, "No matter what, I'll always love you and be here for you. In my eyes, you've always been my son." The damage had already been done though, and those words, I didn't hear. Years later, the characteristics that I saw in my own family and detested were the very ones I came to embody as a means to cover my pain. Again I didn't have a say in my family dysfunction, it's what I was given.

The Broken Piece: Unforgiveness

> To forgive is to set a prisoner free and
> discover that the prisoner was you.

—Lewis B. Swedes

The day I found out about my biological father was the day I went into my prison. These moments in my early years created anger, cynicism, and unforgiveness in my heart toward my family. I had seen what "family" was about in my early years of my life and told myself I didn't want anything to do with them. I was both ashamed and angry with my family for the impact they brought on my life to that point. My family put me in positions that, as a kid, I was unfit to handle, process, or even understand. It felt personal for me, and I had no way of seeing it any other way. The trauma caused by my family only embedded in me the unforgiveness that would push me far away from them as I grew older. I was bitter. Unforgiveness can be defined "when you are unwilling or unable to forgive someone for hurting, betraying, breaking your trust, or causing you intense emotional pain." I never knew it would become my secret prison though. Over the later years, my anger toward my family would flare up and show out, seemingly over small and minute issues. But the damage toward my perspective of family had died many years prior. I began to see my family as I saw everyone else, a potential entity that could harm me and cause pain.

For much of my early years, I was a quiet, observant, and reserved child. I even remember, on one occasion, telling my mother that I was going to do something amazing with my life and that I would never turn out like others in the family. Later in life though, I'd soon inhabit the very traits and qualities I grew up seeing early on in my life. So what happened to me? Like I said earlier, we don't have a choice on who we come from, but we can decide who we become. But what happens when trauma intervenes? I spent years judging my family, often never seeing who I was becoming in the process, not seeing my moments, the moments that were changing the contour of my life.

By the time my teenage years came, I had already seen plenty and was broken enough inside. But it wouldn't just come from the hands of my family and childhood, sometimes trauma comes from all different corners. These last few teenage years would set the tone of my adulthood. It would propel me into a world that would have me searching for something I could never seem to find growing up—myself.

CHAPTER 3

Adolescence

An identity would seem to be arrived at by the way in
which the person faces and uses his experiences.

—James Baldwin

I never experienced death until I was a teenager. I just never expected
it to hit so close to home. I remember waking up to the news that
morning, it numbed my entire body. These last few teenage years of
innocence would be the cataclysmic points that would thrust me into
adulthood without a clear view of the broken permutations that had
been imprinted on my soul.

Death

Through my childhood and teenage years, my family was very
close with another family that lived around the block from us called
the Harts. The Harts had kids about the same age as CJ and I. And
over the years, our families grew close. The Harts had four kids, three
boys named EJ, Eddie, and James, and a daughter named Dede. EJ
was the oldest out of the siblings, and Eddie was next in line. Eddie

and CJ where same in age and grew as close as brothers. I looked at EJ and Eddie as my extended older brothers. James and I were similar in age as well, and became tight friends through the years. Our families spent a lot of time together, often sharing the load between houses of watching us kids. Our families became inseparable, sharing a lot of commonalities between each other, such as religion, family values, lifestyles, and more. Some of my fondest moments as a kid was spending time at the Harts family home, staying up all night playing video games or just hanging outside playing basketball until the street lights came on. It was a regular occurrence for all five of us boys to be together most weekends. CJ and Eddie did everything together—football, birthday parties, freestyle rap, and, from time to time, even get into trouble. They were thick as thieves.

The Harts were like an extended family for me and my brother. But sometimes the quiet tragedy of life disembarks its realities on us when we least expect it. Sometimes we can go from a peak to a valley without ever understanding why. During the time high school came around, tragedy would soon befall our two families and unknowingly separate the family bonds that once were unshakeable. During my sophomore year, Eddie attended a party with a family relative. Eddie was originally supposed to go hang out with my brother that evening but was on restriction from seeing my brother, because weeks prior, my brother and Eddie got into a little trouble. So instead, Eddie went to a party with his cousin. During the party, there was subsequent smoking and drinking that Eddie's cousin participated in. On the drive back home, Eddie was in the passenger seat when the cousin lost control of the car and went off an embankment, killing Eddie instantaneously and the cousin a few hours later in the hospital. The tragic and untimely news sent both our families into shock and heartbreak. "Why?" "How could this be?" "It can't be true." "This isn't happening." These were the countless thoughts that came to my mind that day along with the uncontrollable tears that followed. Both our families were never the same again. "It didn't make sense," I remembered telling myself.

At the time the funeral came around, I didn't even attend. Looking back on it now, I wish I did. My grief and unsettled pain were too much for me to bear. My heart was so broken; I couldn't even shed a tear on the day of the funeral. I lost two of my brothers that day. I remember just sitting on the staircase of my home motionless and with a heavy heart while the rest of my family went to the funeral. I didn't know how to come to grips with the weight of the lost. It was too heavy. And I knew from then on, life would never be the same. I also knew in my heart that I lost more than just Eddie that day, I was losing a part of my family that I knew and grew up with all of my childhood and teenage years. Additionally, I knew my brother CJ was gone. The weight of what I felt that day soon came true. As time would go on, my brother grew completely rebellious, started getting into trouble with the law. Later he'd drop out of high school, leave home, and eventually move out of state. The tragedy changed CJ forever, and my brother was gone. CJ left. It was hard for me, though our family seemed to always be in a state of chaos, my brother was the one thing I had that I could always trust and rely on. Now that constant was no more. I had lost my best friend James, as well as my brother Eddie, the comfort of the Hart family, and now CJ was on his way out.

Brother

Most of us have best friends at one point or another throughout our life. Some still have best friends to this day, others may have lost best friends along the way. The best friend sets above the rest. Best friends have special privileges and permission into our lives that others can't access. Best friends have experienced and journeyed with us in ways that others can't match. The dedication and devotion best friends have to our lives is unquestionable and has been authenticated. The position of best friend isn't given lightly or considered for just anyone. It's not conditional to be only transactional but, instead, based in experiencing the interplay and evolving dynamics within the course of a relationship, such as vulnerability, trust, empathy, humility, and others. My best friend was my older brother. We grew up together in every way, playing sports together, matching Halloween costumes, getting in neighborhood fights together, playing video games, riding bikes, and so much more. Having a best friend as an older brother or sister has its good and bad. My brother could pick on me and terrorize me but also be the first to protect me. My brother easily got on my nerves and did things to upset me, but CJ was there when I was in need. My older brother was someone I knew that I could always count on during my teenage years, but, unfortunately, that would all change. I'd soon be on my own to navigate through these messy waters and rain storms.

CJ had a fair share of challenges. My brother grew up fast and experienced most things in life that a teenager should never have to but did nonetheless. I remember the first time the cops came to our house. I was traumatized watching the cops arrest and take my brother off to jail. I thought I'd never see him again. I even begged the cops not to, I was only twelve and had no clue why the cops were taking my brother to jail. I remember CJ looking back at me, saying, "William, it'll be okay. You'll be okay. Nothing is going to happen to me. I'll be back soon." I cried that whole day. I always looked up to my brother because I never saw him scared. I never saw him afraid of anything. My brother was someone I feared, not because CJ would or could hurt me but out of reverence and approbation for what I knew my brother could do. CJ was well-known and respected throughout our neighborhood. And even in the schools we attended, often people acknowledged me as "CJ's little brother" and respected me as such. I often felt untouchable, knowing that my big brother had such clout and that he would always be around to protect me. That would all change though. The person I always knew to be the constant figure of my safety and protection would be no more. Life sometimes can have a domino effect without us even knowing or seeing it coming. I may have not known my identity, but I knew that as long as I had my brother, I would be okay. But when we lost Eddie, I lost my brother.

Looking back on it now, I never took time to be there for CJ, to be my brother's best friend, to understand my brother's pain. I didn't think to because I always saw CJ as someone that was unbreakable and could handle anything. At times I wish I could be that way, never realizing years later, I actually would. Eddie was my brother's best friend. I still miss Eddie and the Hart family to this day. CJ and Eddie had plan to do so much in life together. My brother's soul lost something after Eddie's death. I lost more of my identity when I lost my brother. CJ eventually left the state and moved to Phoenix, Arizona, while I was left to figure out life during my teenage years alone, recalling those emotions of abandonment all over again. I had to become what my brother used to be for me. CJ couldn't fill that role anymore. Who are we outside the confines of our safety? When left alone, do we know who we are? I ultimately turned to love, but love eventually turned to more pain.

Heartbreak

A year later after my brother had left and moved to Arizona, I had met a girl. It would be the first time I would experience my first ever crushing at the hands of a women. At some point in our lives, we all experienced heartbreak. For some, this will even happen multiple times in life. Heartbreaks come in many forms—a bad breakup, a cheating spouse, loss of a loved one. There are many paths that lead to a broken heart.

It will depend on the stage of life to determine how deep the heartache cuts and the maturity in which we handle it. The painful reality of a heart break is that most of the time, it can have the effect of rerouting our paths in life. Often a heartbreak can be a detriment to the trajectory of our destiny in that it can often blur our visibility in us seeing our possibilities. Sometimes it becomes the only thing that informs our reality. Not only can we not see ourselves clearly, but now we see everything through the lens of a broken heart. It's what sometimes leads to additional broken pieces in our lives. Let's be clear, when I talk about heartbreak, I'm not just talking about someone hurting our feelings or making us feel some type of way. I'm talking about the type of heartbreak that brings us to our knees, crying out with snot running down our face, the heartbreak that hits our inner parts so hard that we can't breathe, the heartbreak that makes our knees want to buckle and make us want to lose our mind. I'm talking about the heartbreak that leads to soaked pillow sheets and comforters from all the tears that were shed, the heartbreak that brings silence to our words, emptiness to our thoughts, and a knife through our heart. I'm talking about a heartbreak that incapacitates our ability to reason with the reality of our life.

When I was in high school, most of the time, I didn't know what I didn't know. Sometimes the means of maturity and growth come by way of experience. And most of the outcomes of said experiences are often out of our control. Unfortunately, this happen to be the story of my life. We're not taught how to handle a broken heart in school. Our parents may even try to warn us about it, but often our maturity is not that developed to sufficiently understand what this would mean emotionally and psychologically. We may even see it in a movie or TV show, but we can't relate to the experience vicariously. Unfortunately, heartbreak can't be an experiment that we can try in advance and say no thanks to. Wouldn't that be nice? Often it comes when we least expect it. My heartbreak came around the time I was in high school, which I'm sure I'm not the only one who experienced this around that time. The effects of that heart break, however, would go on to eradicate my view of women and the value of relationships for the next fifteen-plus years. It's interesting to think how far back we can trace a trauma to when we really begin to breakdown our life.

In high school, my focus was mainly on football, not girls. That changed though. My junior year, I had somehow captured the attention of a young lady named Courtney. I had seen Courtney around the halls a few times and even at pep rallies, never thought much about her though because like I said, it wasn't my focus at the time. Courtney was pretty popular though. Everyone knew her because of her older brother who was a senior at the time. And Courtney herself was a star on the girls' basketball team for our high school. One day we happened to catch each other's eyes in passing during the middle of school periods. We exchanged numbers and of course a few pleasantries, and from there, it was game, set, match.

Courtney and I were inseparable during that year, it seemed—going to almost every school event together, studying together, hanging out at each other's houses, going to movies, and all the others things teenagers do during those years. As time grew, so did our feelings for each other. I never knew enough about what love was at the time to say it, so I never did. But I knew I liked her a lot and that the feelings were mutual—well let's just say I thought they were. Courtney eventually cheated on me with someone I knew, someone I thought was a friend. I remember when Courtney told me everything. We were at my parents' house hanging out that day, and she slipped the famous line, "We need to talk," which we all know what that means. I could tell it was important just by her mood and demeanor that day. As Courtney began to speak, her face welled up with tears. She could barely compose herself and stop crying while she was telling me the story. It was clear, Courtney felt guilty and bad for letting it happen. I became overwhelmed, asking, "Why?" "Why him?" "Why me?" "How could you?" I kept my composure as much as I could through the whole conversation, never showing an ounce of emotion, but my heart was shattered inside. It wasn't just the fact that Courtney cheated on me but that she was breaking up with me at the same time. At the time, I could remember it feeling like I was being stabbed in the heart and then someone taking a gun and shooting me in the same spot. I couldn't believe it. Courtney left my parents' house immediately after telling me. I remember sitting on the floor. After closing the door, I cried out loud, trying to compute what just happened to me as I sat at the bottom of the staircase. It felt as if I was reliving all my trauma—my abandonment, the lie about my father, Eddie gone, and my brother leaving me. Sometimes the worst heartbreaks are the ones that go unexplained, the ones we can't attach any logical reason as to why it happened, so our mind begins to spin and wonder about all the possibilities as to why, often pointing the finger at the only present body—ourselves. I began to challenge and question my very value.

As a teenager, I couldn't quantify the impact those experiences would have on me in the future. It's like the saying that goes "if I knew then what I know now." Back then, I didn't realize the prolong effects and influence pain had on my life when it goes unaddressed, furthermore, how trauma can compound itself by attaching the emotional and psychological effects to existing or new trauma. This is how the tree of trauma grows in our life. The early seeds of my childhood and adolescence were merely the beginning stages of germination, but the constant humidity that produced my tree of trauma to grow emanated from the thunderstorms and hurricanes that life took me through. Long-term, this greatly impacted my ability to cultivate healthy and meaningful relationships. Additionally it caused me to close off that which used to be open. In this case, my heart would never open again after Courtney. I would go on to ensure that I never allowed myself to feel pain from a woman ever again. I told myself it was better to be invulnerable than sitting at the bottom of a staircase, wallowing in tears ever again. I made sure that if anyone was going to be hurt, it wouldn't be me. I would spend the next fifteen years never to be seen, my heart that is.

Prior and during the time of my adolescence, I'd experienced abandonment, almost drowned as a child, learned my parents hid the truth about my real father. My family chaos was a regular occurrence. My parents were on the brink of divorce often. Eddie passed away. The Hart family was no more. My brother was gone. And I had just experienced my first ever heartbreak. The first nineteen years of my life would indeterminately set the stage for the men I would eventually come to hate. Strong words, I know. But at that time, I didn't have a say in my trauma. See, all those moments I was exposed to, I didn't have any other option. Life just happened for me that way, and I was ill-equipped to know what it was, why it was happening, or how to process it or cope with it. Sometimes if we look close enough at the bread crumbs behind us, they'll tell us a great deal of what's ahead of us if we don't begin to close the door of trauma affecting us. As an adolescent, I didn't see my bread crumbs or the roots of my trauma. Had I known what I was experiencing, I might have had a say in who I was becoming. In those first nineteen years of my life, I had cultivated an identity that I didn't have much say in. Sometimes our identity doesn't come by our permission, but rather it gets commissioned through the experiences and vicissitudes of our future mission.

Forming

The late stages of adolescence were a hard time for me. As I said before, I had experienced a lot for the first nineteen years of my life. But after the dust settles and the calm comes after the storms, what was I supposed to do? Who was I supposed to become? What was my identity? These were the questions I had to wrestle with. Teenage years can be tough, having to define values or what values even mean; constantly learning and trying to make good decisions but often failing; making a plan for life, often not even knowing what should be in it; following role models that may or may not be good; continuously developing emotionally, physically, and psychologically with no perfect script on how to do it; and all the while, dealing with the pressure of just trying to keep up with the trends, friends, and reality that comes with life during that time.

It was a perfect storm, and yet, somehow, I had to survive it. I did, but at what cost? I wasn't the type of kid that knew what I wanted to be in life, I only knew and always believed that I was meant for something great. That's what I told my mother so many years before. I knew my life had a purpose, but that's all I knew. What that purpose was though, I had no clue.

For me though, my identity was damaged. I was lost in what I knew to be true. I often felt alone and, on an island, even when I was surrounded by people. I never did confront the pain during my teenage years. It was easier for me to ignore it and accept it as a part of life, not knowing that by avoiding it, I was allowing it to foster additional strains of brokenness along the way. But what was I supposed to do? The only thing I knew I could do was run. Run fast and hit hard, so that's what I did.

Running

I've played sports most of my life. It was the one thing that was always natural for me. I played football, basketball, softball, track, and even tried a little soccer. But I soon realized that with all that running back and forth nonstop, it wasn't for me. Football was my game. I started playing football when I was six years of age. I loved it too. I played a bunch of different positions throughout my football days—from running back, safety, wide receiver, cornerback, line-backer, and even quarterback. I was quite versatile in my abilities, not because I knew the playbook so well or because I wanted to play every position on the field but because of my speed and my ability to not only take a hit but issue a hit as well.

I enjoyed playing football very much. It was fun, but it was also my escape. It was the one thing I could trust in my life to be consistent and enjoyable at the same time. I started playing little league football for the Benson Bruins. I played as an 89er, which is the youngest group of kids, then went on to play with the sweet peas, bantams, midgets, and peewees as I got older. Those were some fun times. The year playing as a midget was the best. Our team went undefeated that year and went on to win the championship. As a kid, it was an incredible feeling, seemed like no one could stop us that year.

From there, I went on to play football in middle school and high school where I became even more popular for my attitude and intensity on the field, as well as my breakaway speed. Often during games, I could hear people shouting, especially my mother, "Just give Will the ball," believing that in my hands and with my speed, I could just somehow make it pass eleven other equally talented individuals and score a touchdown at will or by ease. Sometimes it happened though, and sometimes it didn't. Either way, I just enjoyed being on the field. The field was my second home. I loved football so much as a kid that I would often sleep in my pads the night before a game just to get my head and body in football mode. I was addicted to it, not only playing it but also watching it.

As long as I can remember, my favorite team has always been the Dallas Cowboys, and my favorite all-time player then and still is Emmitt Smith. I did everything I could as a kid to mimic Emmitt's style, but that's not something anyone can or has been able to do over the last few decades. Emmitt truly was a special kind of player. People often give me a hard time about being a Cowboys fan, especially my family, because they know how much of a die-hard fan I am, so much so that my family and friends won't even contact me on a game day because my mood is often based on whether the Cowboys won or lost that day. It's funny thinking about it, but it's been the running joke in my family for years now.

Football was natural for me. It was an escape. I loved it, but it wasn't for me. Does that make sense? Football was my outlet. It was a reality outside of my own internal reality that gave me purpose and identity because I couldn't find it in myself. So often in life, we attach our identity to "entities" because we often don't see significance in ourselves in the light of our predicaments. So the entity or possessions become the bifocals and mecca in which we see and live our lives through.

This was the case for me and football. While everyone saw me as a star and pushed me to take it seriously, I just saw it as a place that allowed me to live safely outside of my circumstances for a few hours. It's often why when I was playing football, I didn't think about college scouts or going to the NFL. No doubt, I probably could've if I had the right outlook back then. But football was like getting outside for recess during school. It was a nice break to get away from my problems for a while. I had pressure to take it serious from my parents, coaches, school staff and friends, but I just didn't see it the way they did.

I always saw football as something fun, something I could run to when I needed to get away, not something I had to do out of obligation or pressure. It's why I continued to play the game because I loved it, but I didn't love it enough to perfect it. I was cocky, angry, arrogant, and lost trying to figure out who I was supposed to become. Football didn't give me that identity either, it just bought me enough time to avoid having to come up with an answer. I found football as a retreat. But inside, I was still in search of finding me, finding my identity, my purpose. I knew I wasn't going to find it in football. But if not that, then who was I to become? Life had dealt me some pretty rough hands before I was twenty. I was heading into young adulthood with an undefined, unsure, and unequipped understanding of myself and my value.

The Broken Piece: Identity

> An identity would seem to be arrived at by the way in
> which the person faces and uses his experiences.

—James Baldwin.

As a teen, this was my conflict, this was my war. I was broken though, so was my childhood, my family, and my teenage years. So I did what I thought made sense. I begin to search and create meaning and an identity for myself. I went out to make my name great. Identity can be defined by "the fact of being who or what a person or thing is." Another reads, "the qualities, beliefs, personality, looks, and/or expressions that make a person or group." The problem was I didn't know what this meant for me.

I had learned in those first few stages of my life that life wasn't going to give me a helping hand. If I wanted anything, then I'd have to go take it no matter who I'd become. I knew it would be better than who I was. I was tired of not having a say in how life affected me. I didn't want to worry about abandonment or my messed-up family or the fact that I didn't know my dad or that I lost Eddie and my brother. I was done with feeling pain and feeling sorry for myself. I had become numb at this point of my life. And in time, Antonious would be born, and William would be no more. From that day on, I'd abandoned everything I knew in search of trying to validate the purpose I always believed I was meant for. But sometimes in search of trying to find ourselves, we end up losing the very thing we were in search of—ourselves. My brokenness didn't end when I was a teenager, those roots that got planted but never got addressed, more where on their way—this time I had a choice. But the path I took would head me closer to a wilderness.

PART 2

Validation

"The action of checking or proving the validity or accuracy
of something, recognition or affirmation that a person or
their feelings or opinions are valid or worthwhile."

CHAPTER 4

Career

The more we value things, the less we value ourselves.

—Bruce Lee

"Remember this, Will, not everything is about you." These were words spoken to me early in my career, but I paid it no attention. After all my first nineteen years had already told me it wasn't about me. Nobody told me who I was or who I could be. What made it worse was that I didn't even know those answers myself. At twenty-one years of age, I found myself as a product of shapeless clay. The only thing I knew for sure was that I wanted to be seen but never fully grasping what that would mean. So I started searching.

Mindset

Life taught me a lot in my early years and a fair amount of pain and trauma to go along with it. I was heading into the real world now with no clue who I was or what I wanted to be in life. Up to that point, life had shown me everything I didn't want for myself. I entered my adult years as a man without values or maybe with the wrong ones. I was out to validate myself without knowing my value. It's interesting to think what becomes of us when we don't see our value from within, I never did.

I was young when I started helping my father with the paper route. I was elated at the opportunity to spend time with him. This was of course before I knew the truth about my biological father. Nevertheless, I enjoyed those earlier mornings with my dad and brother chucking papers around. The job was very simple: make my father proud and help out my family. Nothing about money or being a success was a motivation. Heck, I didn't even understand the depth of those words at that time. It wasn't an exciting or exuberating job to have as a kid my age, but it was a vital part of who I was going to become later on in life. That doesn't always mean it's going to be a straight path though.

We're often told and taught this fairytale that if we work hard, get a good education, stay focused, and stay out of trouble, life should work itself out but were often not told about the many obstacles, hiccups, and possible traumas along the way. The truth is, there is no one constant outside of time. What was once today is gone tomorrow, and what comes tomorrow, we'll never know. There isn't always a perfect straight line to success. But we work hard toward it anyway, often killing ourselves for achievement, triumph, monetary gains, and accolades. We work assiduous for this small settle peace of mind and power. In doing so, we find ourselves overworked, under-appreciated, losing time with people we love while watching life pass us by. Unfortunately, this can lead to regret and an unfulfilled life. But I paid no attention to that. I was out to get my respect. So I began to work for my earthly validation because I was still in search of finding me.

I've always been a hard worker from the time I started that newspaper route with my father to when I became a leader for a technology company later on in life. I did tons of odd and different jobs all along the way, believing that earnest work and dedication would pay off. After all, isn't that the path to the American dream? My first ever job was working at McDonalds. It didn't last too long. In fact, it only lasted a few hours. I quit the same day I started. I refused to be seen in the drive-through window and have my friends just happen to pull up while I was working there. "No thanks," I said and left. I'm sure that was my pride speaking. But even then, I felt I was meant for more. My parents weren't happy at all with my decision. Our house rules were simple back then, "If you live under this roof, you're either going to go to school or get a job," my parents would say. Well I never enjoyed school, but I had no problem getting a job. I wasn't going to settle for just anything though. And so I began to bounce from job to job, trying to figure out what I was going to be. I worked in retail as a cashier; in transportation, loading trucks; in shipping, packing mail crates; in corporate offices as an admin clerk; and soon found myself in technology, working many jobs in an effort to climb the corporate ladder, trying to obtain what I thought success meant. I was trying to create external value without understanding my internal value. I had seen values before. But somehow through all the trauma, I detached myself to what it truly meant.

Model

Hard work through perseverance was a discipline I had demon-strated throughout my life, from my childhood to my teenage years and even in my young adult years. My parents always instilled in us as kids that if we want anything in life, we must work hard for it. My parents have always worked. Even now my dad works while in retirement. I find my father on most days finding projects around the house to keep busy while my mom looks on. That's how my father is, always looking for the next project, never staying still. My father's been working for as long as I can remember. My father graduated from the University of Maryland and after college spent twenty-plus years in the air force and soon after went straight into the workforce, spending the next fifty-plus years building an impressive résumé and providing for our family. And when my father was not in the office, he was in the classroom. My father was also a teacher for fifteen-plus years. My father has always believed in the importance of education. My father showed it as well, earning a doctrines degree later on in life.

My father enjoyed teaching, sharing knowledge, and growing the next generation of individuals to get them prepared for the real life ahead. So I was no stranger to what hard work and discipline meant.

If someone was to ask me about a family story that has inspired me the most, I definitely say "the time my father was laid off," That's correct, I said when my father was laid off. Let me explain. It probably couldn't have come at a worst time in my family's life. My father was an executive at the time, working for Boeing. I was about ten years of age around this time. My parents had recently purchased our first family home, only living in the house for roughly two months when the news hit our doorstep that my father had been laid off. It was a crushing blow to my family, not much was said nor emotions expressed. My mother told us kids, "Things will be tight for a while." I always knew what this meant given our family struggles from time to time. This was a code for "we're on a budget." At the time, my mother wasn't working, instead staying home to take care of the house and us kids. This was heavy news and a huge hit for us that wasn't expected.

I often reminisce about this story and love thinking about it particularly because, for me, this was the first time I had a full understanding and view into what it meant to be a man, father, husband, leader, provider, and protector. Not only did my father get another job to provide for our family and save our home but got three jobs and worked all three each day. My father would wake up every morning at 2:00 or 3:00 a.m. to deliver the newspaper route. This was where I had my first job. my brother and I would go as well sometimes to help out in order to get it done faster. Especially on Sundays, those newspapers were much thicker and took more time to put together. Additionally, the size of the newspaper on Sundays made it impossible to throw like the skinny weekday papers, so we'd have to hand deliver each one to the doorstep. It took hours. Boy, did I hate those Sunday mornings. After completing the newspaper route around 5:00 or 6:00 a.m., my father would hurry home to shower, change clothes, eat breakfast, and head out to his second job at Xerox. My father would get off from Xerox around 4:00 or 5:00 p.m., rush home to grab a bite, and run back out the door to start a night shift at Fred Meyers and wouldn't get off until 11:00 p.m., sometimes midnight. My father would come home, pass out for a little, and do it all over again. This was my model of hard work.

I cry telling this story at times, trying to imagine what my father must have been going through during that time as a man. My father, in the middle of a storm, had to still figure out how to provide and care for our family. My father had to put aside pride and emotions, go into the world, get a job much lower than what I'm sure he deserved, and not just one job but three, just so we could eat. My perspective of my father's values became clear for me since that day: take care of family by any means necessary. During that period, my father showed me that life was about sacrifice and perseverance. That's what my father has always done for my family and even for this country when he served it. Was my father a perfect man? No! Was my father my blood? No! Was he a father? Yes, no question about it.

My father's example of hard work would drive me to be the same in my career. The only problem was I didn't have values like my father did. I didn't know my "why" in life. All I had was my trauma, disappointments, and experiences from my first nineteen years. So I turned to what made sense for me. I turned my attention toward anything to cover my pain and my past: money, power and respect. Though the example my father laid out for me should've kept me on the right path, sometimes our traumas will dictate our perspectives. I went looking for everything I didn't see in my childhood, family, or adolescent years: validation. I needed to validate myself to fill the void left by the untreated trauma and broken pieces in my life, pieces that I didn't know were quietly fueling my identity and decisions, broken pieces that in my twenties I didn't even know were there. I spent the next several years trying to bring validation to the emptiness that was brought on by my brokenness. I just had to find the right crack in the door to make my mark.

Opportunity

I dropped out of high school early in my senior year. I eventually went back and got my diploma. But after learning about my biological father, Eddie's death, the heartbreak, and my brother gone, I lacked motivation and desire to be anything—not an excuse, just the reality of how I thought back then. I'd soon throw out everything I'd been taught by my mother or was shown by my father. I was mad and angry. At the time, I didn't know how to properly handle my emotions or deal with my rage that festered inside me. I'd soon leave my parents' house and set out on my own.

I had a lot of odd jobs throughout my life, especially in the early stages of my career as I tried to define an understanding of what my skills and abilities were. With no college degree or any formal trade, all I had was my perseverance, hustle, and hard work. I had a lot of that. A door would soon open at a technology company where I got the opportunity at a very junior-level position to prove myself. But that was all I needed, just a foot in the door. I learned rapidly and matured my skills in that role in no time. I climbed up the ladder quickly at that company and moved on to duplicate my success at other technology companies.

I was never one of those kids that knew what I wanted to be in life. I didn't want to be a cop, firefighter, artist, musician, doctor, dentist, biologist, or any other several jobs I could list. I didn't want any of those things. To be honest, I was not sure what I wanted to be in life, and that always scared me because everyone else around me seemed so sure of a career choice. But I never felt like I belonged in a box or a category. The idea of picking a career forever and only doing that one job gave me chills and discomfort. "Why just that when I know I could do more?" I would often say to myself. Technology sure wasn't on my mind. I can't recall any time in my early years where I thought of being in that industry. To be honest, I just went in that direction because I saw it could make me a lot of money, and I literally just fell into it. That was the only reason I got into tech and stayed in it: for the money. And thankfully, I became good at it. So I continued to chase the money and power. After all it gave me some sense of peace, happiness, and validation. But it would never fulfill me. Even after I started making six figures, I thought I'd be ecstatic. But then my sight became more, now wanting seven figures. I soon found myself coming to the realization that I was chasing and valuing the wrong things. But if I wasn't in it for money, power, and respect, then what else?

Strategy

Hamdi Ulukaya, CEO of Chobani, said it best in an unapologetic and targeted speech toward business owners. Hamdi went on to say, "The new way of business: It's your employees you take care of first, not the profits. The anti-CEO playbook is about community." Later in TED Talks, Hamdi added, "I am here to tell you no more. It's not right. It's never been right. It's time to admit that the playbook that guided businesses and CEOs for the last forty years is broken. It tells you everything about business except how to be a noble leader. We need a new playbook. We need a new playbook that sees people again, that sees above and beyond profits."

When I first got into technology, I was focused on two things: making money then learning how to make more money. I just wanted to learn. I wanted to learn everything. My father once said, "The key to success is to get in and quickly learn how to do the job you were hired to do, then learn how to do your boss's job." But I don't believe my father was talking about valuing money. I think my father was more so talking about valuing growth and hard work. I took that advise nonetheless and duplicated at many places I worked at. Some point through the process of learning and growing, I was no longer satisfied with just making money, learning and doing a job, and being good at it. I wanted recognition and accolades. I wanted promotion and power. I wanted respect and deeper validation, anything to cover up my pain and my past. I was trying to validate myself through works, not purpose. During my first few years in technology, I went from a junior QA to a leadership role, all within less than two years. I found success fast wherever I went. And while I was developing in my career at a quick pace, I was far off from where I needed to be. But the scary truth was I didn't know where that was exactly.

During the span of my career, I've worked with companies such as Hulu, Amazon, Pokémon, Disney, Fox, Netflix, Roku, iHeartRadio, HBO, HSN, and so many other brands I could list. I've sold and delivered on multimillion-dollar deals and made tons of profits for the organizations I worked for. But at the end of the day, something was still always missing.

There was a time early in my career in tech, I went down to Turner Broadcasting in Atlanta. Turner had come to my company, looking to expand their digital properties onto the Roku platform. The company I was working for at the time wanted me to go down there and put together a pitch and deliver it to Turner. So I flew down to Atlanta with a designer and a solution architect for a few days to put together the pitch.

As my team and I flew down to Atlanta, I had no clue what I was going to deliver or pitch to the Turner team. This was because my company at the time was taking over this opportunity from a prior company that Turner had partnered with, but I wasn't privy to how that relationship ended. Furthermore, I didn't know what Turner was expecting from us. The only thing I had going for me was that I knew everything about Roku, which gave me a little confidence. The other concern, which was the biggest, was that we only had three days to put together the pitch.

On the first day, my team and I spent most of the day in back-to-back, one-on-one meetings with individuals from Turner to investigate and research their current product line to understand their future needs, aspirations, and concerns. The second day, my team and I had to gather everything we had heard the day prior and somehow collect our thoughts, design/define a solution, and come up with a strategy and time line for how we we're going to make their dreams a reality. The next day we had to present.

Walking in the third day, I was 100 percent confident in what my team and I were able to put together in those two days we had prior to going into the pitch meeting, that was until the meeting got underway. When I first got down to the Turner offices on day one,

I was informed that we would be presenting to the product lead at Turner that manages their internal digital TV apps. So heading into the meeting on the third day, I figured my team and I would be meeting with just Marta, that was her name, so it didn't bother me at all to present to Marta, seeing that my team and I met with her repeatedly through the span of those three days. I was pretty confident in doing a pitch to Marta. So when the pitch meeting started on the third day, I figured I sit at the head of the table, seeing how I was going to be doing most of the presenting and talking. As I made it to the meeting that morning, my team and I sat at the table and waited for Marta to arrive. The table was a long conference room table, like one I would find in a boardroom. Marta came in and let us know that a few others would be attending to listen in to our pitch. I was a bit shocked, but, in my head, I figured it would be an additional one or two people. I was wrong. Instead of just one or two people showing up, thirteen people did, all from different parts of Turner and all of them leaders in some capacity. And there I was ignorantly sitting at the head of the table. I felt so stupid at the time. My stomach began to cringe just at the mere thought of presenting to that size of the room as I had only been preparing my mind and even my team for the pitch to Marta.

Needless to say, the pitch went perfect. Turner loved us, and we got the deal. I would go on to do deals and pitches like this many times throughout my career. Some were successful, and others not so much. But my career continued to blossom. Profits would continue to roll in. And overall, my company was happy. But I wasn't. I was still living in the mindset of the old CEO playbook. I was so focused on success, making money and profits, creating a reputation, and getting accolades for myself that I didn't see what truly mattered. My strategy ultimately was about using my career to validate my purpose, never realizing that my very focus was missing the entirety of my purpose. I was in it for me and nothing or no one else. The more success I was having with creating and delivering business results, the more power and respect I wanted, the more I wanted to be promoted and recognized. I was starting to see that what most companies cared about and valued for centuries was the very thing I was becoming: a man solely focused on profiting. My career strategy was to profit the world, but I was slowly losing more of my soul. Sometimes people will come into our life to lend wisdom to our broken values. But if our hearing has been impaired by our past, then our past is all we'll ever hear.

Mentorship

During my tenure at a past technology company, I had the unique opportunity to be mentored by a leader named Russ. Russ and I would meet up once a week and sometimes even more for coffee and chats. It was personal time outside of work hours set aside to discuss my developmental career growth, allow us to get better acquainted, and give me a chance to learn about business. Russ became a mentor and coach for me during this career season of my life. We had some amazing chats, experiences that I'll always cherish. Overtime we developed a close friendship as well. And like any friendship, it had its ups and downs. Russ and I would even blow up on each other at times.

What I haven't mentioned was that Russ wasn't just a mentor for me, he was also the owner of the company that I worked at. Russ had tons of career success as well as general and strategic business experience that intrigued me, which I was able to learn from. I felt grateful that at my age and career level, I was able to get that time with such a leader, and I soaked up everything I could around business, strategy, ethics, leadership, and a lot of other great fundamentals.

As I was continuing to develop in my career path, my desire and passion would elevate past my needs. I soon wanted more leadership opportunities, which I believed I was ready for given all the personal career success I was having. Russ didn't quite agree. Russ said something to me that crushed my spirits and almost caused us to have yet another falling out.

During one of our usual coffee meetups, Russ and I were discussing my career path and leadership opportunities when Russ said to me, "Will, I know you want to be a leader, but I don't think the room is ready for you." When I first heard this, I was upset, irate, and hurt. I never told Russ this at the time, but it devastated me. I couldn't believe the words used. It definitely broke my pride for a few weeks. I also think it changed the dynamic of our relationship because I only listened to the words, I didn't listen to Russ. See, I heard "Will, you're not enough," "Will, you don't deserve it," "Will, we don't want you in there," "Will, you're not worthy of that room." I was hearing everything I felt my past had already told me about myself.

Well I had been missing the whole point from the very beginning. See, when Russ and I we're meeting up for coffee, everything was always about me. I made it always about me and how I could get ahead. Even when Russ said "the room wasn't ready for me," I responded with a very me-centric attitude of "Why not me?" But that was the problem. Leadership isn't about me, it's about serving people, not my own agenda. I wonder if Russ was trying to tell me that I wasn't developed enough to care for others as much as I cared about myself, that I had my values focused on the wrong places. Mentorship is often about developing people, not just for them to attain more but to focus on giving more. Broken values will cause us to have a broken assessment. My values were not aligned to what Russ was teaching me, therefore the perspective was always about me, never seeing that what Russ was really trying to pour into me was a readjustment of my values.

The Broken Piece: Values

The more we value things, the less we value ourselves.

—Bruce Lee

My values were all about money, power, and respect as I said earlier. The money I made influenced my mindset that I could avoid my problems. The power allowed me to feel that I didn't need anyone. The respect I received made it possible for people to truly never see my scars, only my stars, never realizing that having these values was a detriment to throwing away my soul. Values, by definition, is "a person's principles or standards of behavior; one's judgment of what is important in life."

My perception of life and what mattered had been deluded by my past. I was an adult now trying to find what to believe in and, furthermore, what to live my life for. My career only allowed me to further my ability to escape my reality, the validation that my career gave me, filled the void my trauma left me. But there is a backside cost to everything—more broken bread crumbs. It led to my broken values. It led to my inability to make wise decisions and careful considerations regarding my actions and of course my future. When we don't have values, we can become subdued easily by immoral behavior and toxic environments. Since my career didn't validate me and give me purpose throughout the day, I turned to the nightlife. The lack of having the right values in my life led to my poor perception about myself. But my career wasn't my only obstacle into finding new values, there was still other broken pieces that needed a workout.

CHAPTER 5

Fitness

Remember, you have been criticizing yourself for years, and it hasn't worked. Try approving of yourself and see what happens.

—Louise L. Hay

When I started working out, it was for growth and masculinity, never realizing my outward growth reflected my inward decline. My muscles had grown, but my perspective of self was withering away. I was becoming what I thought the world would acknowledge, what the world would validate. But the truth is, I was only covering up the most important part.

Mirror

I was an athlete all my life, a natural athlete. It wasn't too long that I would find a new home to exercise all my testosterone, a home that never really interested me as a kid, a home where we're not often judged by our character or integrity but by our strength and physique. It was the gym where I'd soon realize that my beliefs and esteem were less important than image and appearance, this became my workout.

Like I said, I was an athlete most of my life, but I wasn't no-muscle man. My athletic prowess was my speed, not so much my strength. I was a strong man, don't get me wrong. But when people often thought of me or my physical abilities, it was about my speed. Later on in life though, speed wouldn't be enough for me. I wanted more.

I was in Orlando, Florida, for a week on a business trip at the Disney World Resort, melting in the heat of summer weather, when I decided to hit the gym for the first time during my stay at the hotel. This wasn't because I wanted to enjoy the refreshing air conditioning or because I didn't have anything else to do, it was simply because I didn't like the way I looked in a tank top or without a T-shirt. I remember the moment in my hotel room, looking at myself in the mirror while undressing out of my business attire from my day at the office. I didn't like the image. I wanted to put on a tank top and some shorts, given the summer heat. But my bony body didn't look appealing to me. Before I started working out, I would never wear tank tops, not even in the summer. It was always T-shirts. I just always felt inferior to others inside of my own skin. Additionally, I had hypertrophic burn scars on my body from that childhood incident that embarrassed me. Sad, I know. But many people today have low opinions of themselves that constitute foolish beliefs and behaviors. I noticed what I thought others would notice, and that was simply that I wasn't enough. I didn't look the part, somewhere inside of me was a self-belief of comparing what culture appealed to when it came to physique against the reality of my own physical masculinity. I felt like I didn't measure up. This was an additive view of how I saw myself, given the early roots of my trauma.

During my first of what would become many workout sessions, I was simply a person trying to figure out how to work the machines, what workouts I should be doing, and how much weight I could possibly lift. Every workout only intensified my desire to learn and push myself more. I had no workout routine, regiment, or goal. For me, it was simple: push more weight, begin to look great, and soon get the body that society wants. That whole week, I found myself working out at the mini hotel gym after the work day. By the time I left to go home once my business trip was concluded, I was hooked. I wanted be as strong as I was fast. I wanted to be seen in a different light. Before my flight reached back home, I had already made up my mind that I was going to get a gym membership. By the time the next day came, I was up at the local LA Fitness doing just that. I'd spend the next eight years working toward that one simple concept: "Push more weight, begin to look great."

When I first started working out regularly at the gym, I was there six days a week for three hours at a time. A little much, wouldn't we all say. I was addicted. I still had no workout routine and never bothered creating one. Every day I showed up, deciding what body part to work on. There would be some days I would just workout the whole body. My body was resilient as well, I hardly felt sore or tired after my workouts. There were a few days where I could do the same body part back-to-back.

I wasn't the most social person when it came to being at the gym either. I was focused, determine, and consistent about getting my physique. I wasn't in it to make friends or become a fitness expert, I was about gains. That was it. My consistency and work ethic though made me appear to others. Often people were asking me those basic routine gym questions like "how long you been working out?" "Do you compete?" "What kind of workout plan do you follow?" But I would just say, "There aren't any shortcuts, need to put in the work." I showed very little respect to others in the gym, often seeing myself better than people because of how hard I worked. Additionally, people didn't know or realize that I didn't know half the workouts I was doing or what body part I was working out. My concept of working out wasn't based on what others had done before me. It wasn't based on reading a magazine or a training plan. It wasn't based on a certain weight or physique. I just knew the more I lifted those weights, the stronger I would get, and the better I would look. My internal dislike of myself was the external fuel that pushed me. I just knew I didn't like what I saw in the mirror. I was a man on a mission. Sometimes I wonder if I knew exactly what mission accomplished looked like for me.

As the days and years went by, I would start to notice something very strange, something that I never realized throughout all those years of training. I noticed that every time I looked in the mirror, I saw the same person I did that week in Orlando when I first started my workout journey. I saw that I didn't fit in, that I didn't measure up. I felt I was missing a moving target every time, and I didn't know why. Sometimes the mirrors we look through don't show us our real view. I had biceps, triceps, a huge back, nice chest, strong legs, shoulders that look like I could carry the world on them, yet I still felt insufficient. How's that possible? After all the hours, days, weeks, and years at it, could I feel this way? Why did I still feel inadequate when I had the physique that most people only dream to have? My new appearance didn't change my reality, it only distorted my mentality.

Ego

My size and muscle strength came quickly for me. I still wasn't wearing tank tops and running around without T-shirts, but I was enjoying the progress nonetheless. As my muscle mass would grow, friends and family would start asking questions or insinuating that I was taking enhancements, steroids, or something of the sort. Because my friends and family weren't in the gym or spending the countless hours and days sweating it out with me, people didn't believe that my transformation was all natural. It would upset me that people would think I would ever go that far to get results, but I'd ignore it because I always knew how much I was putting into it. Soon after, friends and family forgot about the speedy little kid who once ran laps around people. I was now seen as some kind of incredible hulk. It felt good.

As the muscles took form, so did my new-found attitude, ego, and confidence. I was always a confident person to some degree, but I carried it differently now that I had the arms and body to go with it. I was starting to see how much attention I was garnering simply by how I looked. Even when I would go shopping or out to dinner, people would ask me if I was a football player or fitness trainer. Though I'd tell my friends and family that I didn't like the attention, inside it was feeding my ego with every compliment or look I would get. Over the years, my intensity never wavered when it came to the gym. My attitude was the same every year. There was never a goal set for me to achieve, it was all about pushing weight and pushing myself to be better than weeks prior. The gym became my new football field. If I'm being honest, I never had any goals set because it was never truly about physique and beauty. Those were only manifestations of an internal cancer. The root of it was all about my low self-esteem.

It's actually because of my self-esteem issues that I got kicked out of the gym where I first started my workout journey. There was another guy that would come to the gym almost as much as I would. His name was Earl. Earl was a body builder and never tried to hide it. Earl was often seen posing in the mirror, flexing his pecks, and taking pictures of himself. Anytime Earl lifted weights, he was super loud about it and caused most people to stop and give attention to his workouts. From the very beginning, Earl and I didn't like each other. I'm not sure why. I'm assuming with all the testosterone in that building and both of us vying for results, I guess we saw each other as competition. I know I did. From the moment I saw him, I didn't like him, I had no reason not to like him. But my lack of self-esteem mixed with my ego only allowed for anger and jealousy to set in.

On one late night workout though, I had enough of this macho ego stuff. I wanted to truly test how much of a man he was, not just when it came to weight lifting but when it came to throwing those hands. I grew up fighting. Plus being raised around my brother, I wasn't afraid of anything or anybody, no matter how big they were or what they had on them. Earl and I would always give each other some kind of dirty look or attitude, but on this one night, I had enough of it. Earl was working out around the same area I was in and was making a lot of noise and taking his usual selfies, and that was enough for me to set it off. I approached him and said a few expletives and told him I was tired of him thinking that he was someone that people needed to fear and that I had no problem knocking him out if he wanted to go at it. Earl's face said it all, he seemed shocked and confused. Earl wanted to talk it out and defuse it. He kept saying, "I don't want to have any problem with you," but I kept taunting him to fight. Eventually the gym staff and other people stepped in to break it up. And soon later, they had kicked me out the gym and banned me from the facility.

Truth is, my problem was never with Earl, it was with myself. It was how I saw myself: inferior. But my ego wouldn't allow me to see the truth. My ego wouldn't allow me to see another broken piece.

Self

Ever wondered how it's possible that in a world with a gazillion people inhabiting our planet each and every day, why are we the only people of our kind? How is it possible that there is only one "us"? Can it be that everything about us is that inimitable that no single person can take or duplicate our form? Every part of who we are was intricately created, designed, and assigned for us from our physical form all the way to our genetic code, from the way we laugh to the way we cry, from the way we love to the way we hurt, from the way we think to the way we feel, from the way we smile to the way we frown, from the way we talk to the way we walk, We are the way we've been fitted to be. We are beautiful. We are timeless. We are exclusive. We are a limited edition. We are one of kind. We are irreplaceable. We are a walking miracle. That's us. So why did I spend so much of my life in hiding? Why did I allow my brokenness or society's views to determine the value of my very essence? Where did I lose the meaning of "self"?

I was speaking with a friend named Ennis over dinner one night. Ennis began telling me about an idea to build a business around all of her person passions. Ennis articulated to me that people were following her on social media, specifically the content showcasing the five unique services based on her passions. Ennis conveyed to me how people were starting to want more of that content and how she began realizing her services were uncovering a need in our society. Ennis came to me needing my help to figure out a business model but also a brand that would encompass all the aspects of her passions and values that people came to love. As Ennis continued to walk me through her thoughts, which I have to admit, half the time I was completely lost trying to figure it all out which Ennis could tell—not her fault. Ennis has a deep, creative, and intricate mind. And honestly, her thinking at times is from another planet, while I'm still on earth looking at her saying, "Huh, what was that?"

As I sat there listening intently to Ennis's passions, not her words, she continued to communicate to me the challenges in defining the business, given how set apart her services were from each other. Ennis also communicated the struggle to figure out a way to distinguish the unique value proposition to a specific brand identity. I begin to lead Ennis on this journey, to breakdown who Ennis was as a person and why she was doing all this in the first place. Ennis proceeded to tell me how this came about through the experiences of writing her dissertation and going through her own personal life experiences. Ennis communicated that she had to get to a place where she loved herself again despite the broken marriage, the dysfunction in her family, and other outliers that she endured. Ennis's ability to love herself despite what life had served her was crucial in her messaging. Ennis continued to tell me that she had a concept called self-love that she was using for some other side project.

As I begin to think about everything Ennis told me over the course of our dinner and about all she experienced, it was clear that the services were in direct correlation to her story, that the idea of self-love was the one constant that tied it altogether. That self-love was the very brand that Ennis encompassed. Ennis was in the business of self-love. As I walked away from our dinner feeling good about our conversation and how I was able to help Ennis think through her business concept, I was unsettled at the idea that here I have a friend that was creating a business around helping others to love themselves. It bothered me deeply. While I loved the idea and supported Ennis's intentions to drive this message and value home for our society, I began asking myself, "What happen to us as people? How have we strayed so far away from our own identity that we now need apps or some kind of technology to remind us of who we are? Why have we become so disgusted with our own reality that we'll trade it for the smallest margin of pretentious and counterfeit validation out there?"

It wasn't until a few days later, I realized that Ennis's business idea was speaking directly to me.

When I decided to hit the gym, it wasn't out of excitement to lift weight or to do tons of cardio, it wasn't to get on some extraordinary workout plan or some nutritional diet schedule, and it sure wasn't to spend hours upon hours exhausting myself to sweat and smell like I'd been running through a Sahara. It was simply because I looked out around myself and saw everything that I wasn't. Ever wonder why we have eyes that only look outwardly, but our biggest issues come from within us? Can we really not see us? I was allowing perception to blur my perspective of what really mattered. I started voiding my very distinct inherited essence to fit into a false reality.

Society

I feel that we live in a world today that our obscurity is devalued for the sake of notoriety no matter the cost. When I started out, my concept was to push more weight, begin to look great. But why? What would that achieve for me? How would that change how I saw myself? While I saw a modern world that was driven by social media, tied around image and appearance, I didn't understand how I fit in with it. I didn't even do social media back then. In fact I hated it for just that reason, because to me, it felt unauthentic and presented a false narrative of who people really are or what people really go through. But I guess to some degree, I still lived in the mindset of social media. I just didn't do it online, I did it with life. I knew I was obscure, but I didn't want to go unseen. I felt like everything around me was telling me that to fit in and to be of importance, I had to look a certain way. No one told me this, but sometimes our pain or our past will tell us lies.

As I look out at the world today, I see most of our culture turning into followers without a clear identification of who the leaders are. I see continuous trends that push more about image, appearance, how we look, what we should wear, and how we should present ourselves while hardly ever addressing the man or woman on the inside.

Does it matter though? Does integrity, honesty, loyalty, discipline, empathy, or character even matter to people anymore? Can we spot it if we saw it? Would others follow it?

I feel we have a herd mentality when it comes to our culture today. We'll lose ourselves just so we can run with the pack in the hopes of being seen. We'll follow a trend or a person just so that we can be tied to someone or something of greater value than we see in ourselves. Almost everything around us is telling us that we don't measure up. We're always being sold more of something because who we are or what we have just isn't enough. It's everywhere. It's on billboards, magazines, newspapers, social media, television commercials, news feeds, or plastered on the side of buses. We have influencers and business leaders pushing all these ideals of what we need to do to be a better person, earn more income, look more appealing, get more followers, and so on. Don't get me wrong, I'm all about promoting ideals that help individuals grow but not at the expense of us losing our soul or the very intricate piece that sets us apart. I was chasing esteem. And by doing this, I lost myself even more. People loved and gravitated to my looks but never really saw me. Looking like a muscle head and acting like one was all I came to know. I had been doing it for so long. We may not like our physical appearance or the way our body looks in particular outfits or clothing, and that's fair. We must be sure when we look in the mirror that we always still see ourselves, our true selves, not someone else or some trend we're trying to live up too.

Oliver Jones, a British artist, decided to do a series of drawings exploring society's obsession with perfect skin. Part of Oliver's inspiration came from the slogan that the skin care company Olay uses for a slew of marketing campaigns: "Love the skin you're in." In one of the series drawings, Oliver has one of the most captivating images, it's one that features his baby daughter Eve, marked up with plastic surgery lines around her face. The picture is entitled "Maybe She's Born with It." In an interview Oliver did shortly after, he was quoted making the following statement: "We often forget or oversee that how we actually experience flash in every day, in the mirror, from the supermarket shelves, and through the routines we put in place to maintain or improve it are far removed from industry's portrayal."

Oliver goes on later to say, "Society has never been so saturated with images of flesh (particularly images of the face) that have been produced and altered in a way that emits an aura and notion of perfectionism or a vision that we should strive to achieve."

This isn't going away. If anything, this notion and vision is being released more and more each day through our society. If we're not careful, we'll fall into its trap. I fell into it, and the sad part was that I didn't even know I was stuck in that hole. I'm here to convey that real muscle, real strength, real sexiness and beauty lives on the inside, lives inside of each of us. Our workout is in how we see ourselves and what we say about ourselves every day. That's the work. That's our real gym.

The Broken Piece: Self-Esteem

Remember, you have been criticizing yourself for years, and it hasn't worked. Try approving of yourself and see what happens.

—Louise L. Hay

Every time I looked in the mirror, I saw something wrong with the picture. I never approved of myself.

It's important to understand the difference between self-worth and self-esteem. While at times they're used interchangeably, it's important to recognize these words have entirely different meanings. Self-esteem focuses on how we assess and evaluate ourselves, how we judge our potential qualities and attributes and the acceptance of our own reality. Self-worth is interdependent of our traits and qualities, "it's the belief that we are lovable and valuable as a person to those around us." It's important to manage both of these coherently through life. I never identified my intentions. While I didn't like what I saw in the mirror, I never questioned what was wrong with it or why was it a problem. I didn't get to the root of my why. It was easier to follow the trend, to follow the herd, to move away from obscurity and inch closer to notoriety.

My biggest problem was that I never saw myself. I had a moment. Looking through that mirror, I realized that no matter how hard I worked to appeal to the masses, society would never see the real me. Furthermore I concluded that the real workout I needed to tend to was the one that the mirror couldn't see, the one thing that truly mattered: myself. I wasn't wrong for thinking that I wasn't enough. I couldn't see myself otherwise. I was continuing to search for validation to place in the cracks of my broken pieces. My outlook had been distorted by all that I was seeing and believing to be real quality in our world. I never healed my outlook. So when I looked in the mirror, I always saw the same reflection.

Sometimes our greatest moments of growth can be found in standby. I spent so many years investing on the physical and looking at what was going on around me that I never looked inside of myself to see the real mess. I overinvested in the wrong area of my life. It's okay, it happens. We must be careful where we invest our time, energy, and our resources. Time is the most valuable commodity that we can't get back, so we must be careful on what we spend it on. My low self-esteem and image of myself only led me to seek more validation. But this time, I didn't look for it in my career or in the gym. I started to search for light in the dark.

CHAPTER 6

Nightclub

We cannot think of being acceptable to others until
we have first proven acceptable to ourselves.

—Malcolm X

I was in darkness trying to find light, but it only seemed to get more
darker by night. My daytime was merely the routine of life, I came
alive at night. The night brought me to a place the day could never
provide me. It was in the night that my life became dark.

Routine

It was Friday, the closing of yet another long week at the office.
This was the day I looked forward to all week. The weekend was
here, three days of fun, relaxation, and space to clear my head from
an exhausting week. As a single man living in my own bachelor pad,
making good money, the weekends were all about having fun. By the
time Friday nights even hit, my plans were already set to meet up for
dinner and drinks with friends before heading out to the clubs. I'd
usually start getting ready around 6:00 p.m.

My routine was always the same: start my night by pouring a nice tall glass of Southern Comfort, Hennessey, or Patron. Depending on how my week ended would define what liquor I'd drink for the evening. Once I took a few sips, it was off to get ready. First I had to shave the head, trim the beard, and brush the teeth, then off to a nice hot and cold shower—hot to wash up and cold to cool off. Once out of the shower, I'd put on some deodorant, lotion, and cologne but not much because I would add more on before leaving the house. I'd usually figure out what I wanted to wear that night while I was in the shower. This way, I could get dressed quickly. Once dressed, I'd head back to the kitchen for a few more sips and often another glass of liquor, return a few calls or text messages that I'd missed, and listen to a little music to set the mood. Once 8:00 p.m. rolled around, I would spray a little more cologne on, put on my jewelry, grab my kicks, check myself out in the mirror one last time to make sure everything looked exactly how I envisioned, and get ready to head out.

As I head out, I would double-check to ensure I got everything I needed for the night ahead of me. I would grab the keys, wallet, phones, and any other essential items. I was ready for a night out. I'd hook up with my friends for dinner. It was usually smiling and laughter as we downloaded and converse about everything going on in our lives. However our discussions usually would lead to us talking about our plans for the evening and more so our intentions. Whether my friends were single, in a relationship, or married, if we were going out to the club, we had intentions. Good or bad was beside the point.

As I would wrap up dinner and drinks with my friends, it was time to head to the main part of the night, this was where all the action takes place, where moments were created, where decisions were made, where people were judged, where integrity was dismissed, where values were ignored, where petulance derived, where inhibitions were explored, and where, for short few hours, our self-worth was the commodity in which we trade on. What we trade it for was often the question that validated not only our moral compass but also exposed the desolates of our hearts.

Once I got to the club, I always parked far away from it. It tended to get a bit rowdy after the club, so it was always best to park farthest from it just to be safe. As I made my way to the entrance, I could hear the music beginning to stimulate my senses as I would start to imagine the fun my friends and I were about to enjoy. Depending on the relative "nightlife" status or celebrity, most people would either have to stand in line and wait to be checked in, or if well-known to the club owners and security, it would be easy to skip the line and head in. I never waited in line. I knew pretty much every owner or head security person at all the swanky clubs.

Once I was inside, after skipping past the long lines of course, I would quickly take a moment or two to glance at the scene I spent the whole night thinking about and imagining. Depending on the club, I'd make my usually trips around the establishment; say hi to the bartenders and barbacks; check on the security guys, most of which were personal friends; give hugs to the cocktail waitresses; stop by the DJ booth to show some love; then head straight back to the bar for drinks or my reserved table to drink as the music pounded the walls of the edifice. In the club, there was always something to see: people dancing; socializing; drinking or ordering drinks; individuals standing around, looking for the next potential bad relationship, hookup, or future wife or husband; women dressed often in scantily and revealing clothing; men aggressively vying for women's attention; while others in groups to celebrate a birthday, anniversary, engagement, or any other kind of special celebration for the evening. The night was full of many indulgences, which often allowed me to forget the problems left at the doorsteps of my home and in the backyard of my soul. This was the place where I'd secretly compete against the threshing floor of my own identity and value, often comparing it to the subject matter of the environment. The nightclub was the place where I often couldn't see people but pretenders, masking their true identities in hopes to be seen and possibly validated. I was one of them.

As the night would end, it was time to find my way to the next spot that may be an after-hours party, a late-night restaurant to eat, home to get in bed or someone else's bed, or find my way to the nearest restroom to release myself from the night's intakes. Most often, the way my night ends didn't always align to how it began.

The nightlife offered me three things: escape, exposure, and excess. But like most things, there was always a backside to it, available to those that come looking for it. I spent most of my twenties in the environment of this lifestyle. It was the scene that gave me the space to be everything that people would come to respect, as well as allow to hide the true person I could never accept: myself. I spent over a decade living in this world, trading my values and very essence for momentary man-made exaltation.

Lifestyle

I started getting into the nightlife scene around the age of twenty-three. A couple of years later, it would become like my second home, my hidden world, and a completely different lifestyle, attitude, and persona that I'd come into outside of my everyday life. I made new friends, family, routines, traditions, associations, reputation, and much more that was completely disconnected from who I was during the day. The night was a different spotlight for me. Some might even say it was a completely different character. It was though. I became two different people. It was simply that I didn't want my day life to converge with my nightlife. I didn't want my past to converge with my present. Like I said earlier, the nightlife offered me three things: escape, exposure, and excess.

The nightlife for me was an escape from the reality of what my life presented for me. For most people, we are always trying to escape something. It could be a broken home, a dysfunctional relationship or family, a purposeless life, loneliness, unsatisfied career, parenting, unpaid bills and debt, recent loss of a friend or love one, boring homelife, and I'm sure I could list many more. The nightlife allowed me to escape all that reality for a few hours and live carelessly into the night, only to find my problems right where I left them.

The backside of escaping my problems and my traumas was that I grew further away from the root cause of my pain. My escaping only deepened my demons. I was running toward everything my life was not during the day, only to try and hope that through the night,

I could find some semblance of meaning, purpose, and validation. For me, this wasn't just a night out on the town, this was about trying to establish an identity that would validate my self-worth in a world that I saw was better than my own. I wanted a way out. I needed to escape my world. I needed to escape my reality. I needed to escape my unsatisfied career, my dysfunctional family, loss of friends and loved ones, my low self-esteem, my broken relationships, and my broken pieces. How many of us are doing this today? What are we trying to escape? I was simply trying to escape a life that had no purpose, a life that had no meaning, a life where I felt that I didn't matter.

This wasn't only an escape for me, it was also exposure. Often living in the nightlife, I could expose myself in a way that allowed others to see me as I would like to be seen. Everyone loves attention, right? But what happens when that attention we seek or validation we desire isn't getting fulfilled in our daily lives? The nightlife allowed me to become whoever I wanted. The exposure put me in the limelight. It gave me a reputation, an identity, and a passport to get the attention I needed. I became the very thing I was exposed to, so much so that people visiting the clubs would often ask me if I worked there, given my persona and how I was treated by staff and partygoers. I'd get free drinks from bartenders, tons of attention from people, hookup with VIP, access into places regular attendees didn't have, and, of course, never had to wait in line. I was a regular. When I had that type of exposure, people started seeing me and treating me differently than how I got treated at home or on my 9:00 to 5:00. It fed me differently. It validated my self-worth.

There was a backside to it. While I was getting the attention and validation from the exposure, I was also becoming the very thing as well. People really never saw me or knew me, the depth of meaning and value was only on the surface, through my persona. Additionally, I lost my sense of self even more because I spent so much time trying to have a rep, I traded my worth. I wanted exposure, but it led to losing my authenticity only to gain momentary endorsement. What are we wanting others to see that we're willing to trade our worth? What attention are we seeking? I wanted to be seen, to be important, but this world didn't just give me escape and exposure, it gave me excess—excess of every kind; sex, drugs, alcohol, and sometimes even violence. For me, this was everything when it came to nightlife. The excess was endless in this lifestyle, especially the longer I stayed in it. With me, alcohol and women were my addiction, often getting so hammered that I wouldn't pass a Breathalyzer test if I was given one after a night out. Often because of my ego, I would still drive back home drunk on many occasions. Often in this lifestyle, it's the sex, drugs, and alcohol that brings all the people together, not that we're all indulging in it of course, but it's often the common denominator for why we're out in some way or another. Not for everyone though, many are content with just going out to listen to some music, dancing a bit, hanging out with close friends, and calling it a night. I'm more so speaking to the men or women that make the nightclubs a weekend tradition. And I wasn't just going out on the weekends, it was almost every night during the week. I always found myself at some club or bar, drinking the night away. My excess only furthered my escape and more so my reality. When it came to women, the excess was even worst. Almost every night, my objective was to find a new woman to meet and have sex with. Sometimes not even making it home to enjoy such indulgences, I'd have sex with women right in the club in the backroom of the owners or security offices. The club for me was like the old Burger King slogan, "have it your way," and that's exactly what I did. At the club, there was always opportunity to hook up with a new woman because there were always new options with every occasion. This excess filled the void of my loneliness and covered my issues of abandonment.

The backside of excess is too much of it, not just the drugs, alcohol, and sex, but even the lifestyle of living in the nightlife can impair the judgments we make about our actual life. For many in this lifestyle, if we're not careful, the excess will lead us to a quick rest, the kind we don't wake up from, the rest that comes with peace, if you know what I mean. I knew this as I saw many of my friends or people I knew wind up dead because of living in this lifestyle—whether it was from drug overdoses, car accidents from drunk driving, alcohol poisoning, or shootings—the excess put their life on the express track toward a tragic and heart-wrenching death. But it's not just the excess of drugs and alcohol that we should be careful with, it's also the lifestyle itself and the addictive nature it presents. I often found myself running to this lifestyle or other tainted routines because I didn't see purpose in myself. I didn't believe in my own value or worth. I lost myself to momentary fulfillments, chasing man's acceptance and worldly validation which became the very distraction from my purpose. I was becoming a product of the wrong environments.

Birthday

I was turning twenty-eight years old, and like every birthday, I spent it throwing a huge celebration. It would always start with a dinner at a classy restaurant and then a night out to my favorite club to enjoy my reserved table and endless bottles of alcohol. My birthdays were always emotional for me because often, I found myself reflecting on another year of regret and shame. But instead of confronting that mess, I would throw these celebrations with friends and family, again, as another way to escape my life. I was in a relationship at this time, so I knew that I could drink up with my friends and enjoy my night as I knew my girlfriend was my designated driver for the evening. Of course in mind, this allowed me to indulge in all my usual excesses.

After dinner, we got to the club and headed upstairs to the VIP area of the club where my table was. My girlfriend told me that she would sit there with the girls and hang out and told me to go enjoy my night with my friends. That was exactly what I did, but I went a little too far. While my girlfriend was upstairs enjoying her friends, the music, and the ambiance of the evening, I was running around the club taking shots and hanging out with my friends and other partygoers. I eventually found myself downstairs at the bar toward the back of the club venue. My girlfriend came down once or twice to check on me but would quickly head back upstairs once she knew that I was okay.

It was around 1:00 a.m. when the club became so packed that people could barely move around the atmosphere. My girlfriend was still upstairs watching over the table and hanging out with her friends. Once again, I found myself downstairs partying at the back bar while friends and random people buy me shots. I ended up meeting a girl, and we started talking and drinking together out of celebration for my birthday. I quickly forgot that I was in a relationship and that my girlfriend was literally in the same venue as I was. Needless to say, this girl and I became attracted to each other right away and didn't waste any time showing it. I'm sure the alcohol helped with that a little. I signaled to the bartender to unlock the backdoor office that was located behind the bar. I went in the back office with the girl, had sex, and went back to my birthday celebration as if nothing happened. My girlfriend never knew or found out, and I sure never told her. It was one of many secrets I would keep throughout the years. But nonetheless, this was who I was during this season of my life. This was what the lifestyle allotted me, not to mention my broken values that lent to my poor judgment in decisions. The nightlife allowed me to live in darkness and hide it all at the same time.

Imposter

John Wimber once said, "Show me where you spend your time, money, and energy, and I'll tell you what you worship." The nightclub became my place of worship, so I traded my worth simply so I could escape, get exposure, and enjoy the excess that presented itself.

I lost who I was because my worth was no longer tied to me knowing and accepting myself but rather allowing the exposure of my environments to validate who I was, to validate my very worth. Who do we become when we don't know our worth? What do we have to put on to hide who we are because we've lost knowing our worth? The answers were easy for me, either someone else or something else. I often became what I saw, envied, or were being exposed to as a result of not falling in love enough with who I was. I began telling myself and believing the lie that it was better to be what I was not than to be who I was, because often I didn't feel enough. It was these thoughts and lies that led me to become something or someone I was never meant to become all because I didn't love myself enough—the good and the bad parts.

This is why we must be present enough to see our hearts at work, in the environment we spend our time in, and really wrestle with the authenticity of our character in those places. I had put on a lot: clothes, personality, fluidity of my articulation, attitude, persona, and much more. But if I'm honest, I did this everywhere, whether it was in the gym wearing clothes to show off my muscles; at the church, acting holier than thou and wearing my religious traditions; at the office, trying to compete with coworkers to be seen by the higher ups; at the club with my best clothes on, acting like I had it altogether. But once I got home and took all that off and stood naked in the mirror, what did I see? Who did I see? That was my problem. These broken pieces led me to lose my worth.

The Broken Piece: Self-Worth

> We cannot think of being acceptable to others until
> we have first proven acceptable to ourselves.
>
> —Malcolm X

Have we accepted ourselves? Better yet, have we accepted everything that has happened in our life up to this point, the good and the bad, the blessings and the curses, the triumphs and traumas? I never did. So I couldn't truly love myself, therefore I couldn't truly know my worth. This is where I lost myself. *Self-worth*, by definition, "is the opinion you have about yourself and the value you place on yourself."

This broken piece was a huge one for me, not because of its significant depth and harm to my internal soul but more so because of the time I spent throwing away my worth and who I became in the process. I spent over a decade in a lifestyle and in patterns because I didn't know my worth. I traded the wealth of my worth for the validation of man and society.

Antonious would be born during this season. While I experienced a season of chasing validation as a means to cover my trauma in parallel to my career, the gym, and the nightlife, I became lost. The years I spent trying to find meaning and my purpose in the world only led me to more destruction and desolation. It led me to a wilderness, not knowing who I was; led me to greater suffering, heartache, and mistakes that I never saw coming. It would become the season of my great downfall.

PART 3

Lost

"Unable to find one's way, not knowing one's whereabouts, missing or unable to be found, or it can mean something that was wasted or not used in a valuable way; can't be recovered."

CHAPTER 7

Criminal

Where there is anger, there is always pain underneath.

—Eckhart Tolle

My hate for myself fueled my fury toward the world. My heart had been sitting on the stove for so long, I never saw the fire raging underneath. Everyone saw the front side of my life through my career, the gym, or in the nightclub, but no one saw the backside of my secret anguish that was tearing beneath the surface of my humanity. I had hidden demons that were betting on my soul. This season of my life would set me on the brink of losing my life. I didn't plan to end up like this. I never planned to take my own life, but I never saw that I had lost it many years prior.

Emotions

Most, if not all of us, are filled up with pain and trauma of some sort that have gone untreated. Many of us have allowed our untreated issues to come out in different manners, not realizing that often, our outburst is connected to the very pain that has gone on untreated. Pain always has the ability to speak on our behalf, especially the deep pain that has gone ignored. As a man, this was more prevalent for me as well, given my propense inability to confront my emotions while allowing my anger to boil over a heated stove. Most often, anger is the only emotion we, as men, know how to display because we don't properly know how to speak effectively to the issues going on inside of us. Yelling and screaming seem like the easiest and quickest reaction we rely on to achieve our results. Unfortunately by doing this, we never win the war. We most certainly lose the battle. But most importantly, we continue to kill our souls. When we deprive our hearts and conceal our pain, we only create the ability to fill our capacity with more anger. The validation I was seeking in my career, by hitting the gym or by going out to the nightclubs, never filled my void or resolved my pain and trauma. However it directed my empty capacity toward anger, malice, and poor decisions.

Silence

"How did I become so angry?" "What's driving my thoughts?" "Is this the person that I wanted to be?" "How did I allow my anger to become a part of my story and get in the way of my destiny?" I considered these thoughts and more as I wrestled with myself, taking time to reflect on my life on one quiet evening, reflecting on the entirety of where my life had brought me. Sometimes who we want to become and who we actually turn into happen in the quiet and quant places of our souls. Its only through time and experiences do they begin to harden into the subtle parts of our character that even our closest friends, associates, and ourselves don't see happening at times.

So how did I, a simple kid who grew up playing toy cars and video games, turn into someone who became immune to criminal activity and chaos as if I never saw it coming? I was a quiet kid, always doing more observing than talking, never one who tried to fit in or hang out with the cool kids. I was the type to keep to myself, never one to exhibit a lot of emotion either. Often for most people,

I was hard to read. I didn't smile a lot and wasn't one to always open up and say what was on my mind. It's not that I didn't want to or didn't have anything to say. I simply didn't know how to connect with people. I didn't know, not because I was socially awkward or had a disability of some sort but because I didn't trust people not to hurt me. Those broken pieces in my first nineteen years taught me not to get close to people.

Throughout my life—from childhood, adolescence, and even as an adult—I faced trauma and pain of many kinds. But for me and like most men, we bury our pain. We hide our emotions. We suffocate our voice before we cry out for any help. This is where I lived. Better yet this is where the embryo of my anger began, where the birth of my violence was manifested.

In time, my pain would begin to speak for itself through anger and rage, later would turn into violence. I filled myself with lots of anger through the years, and it came out often, whether it was yelling at my parents, getting in fights in school, treating women like disposable garbage, threatening people's lives, blowing up on supervisors or coworkers in the office, fighting with teammates on the football field, getting in bar brawls, or even knocking people out just for looking at me the wrong way. I seemed to carry a chip on my shoulder everywhere I went. The questions from friends and family begin to pose themselves, such as "Why is Will so angry all the time?" "Why doesn't Will ever smile?" "Why does Will seem so serious?" Sometimes who we really want to be is hidden behind the things we don't say. Often people judge the frown without caring to hear the inner architecture of pain that built the grimace. Throughout the stages of our lives, we are experiencing life, developing ourselves, and shaping our capacity along the way. I wanted to speak, but I didn't have the capacity for it.

Alcohol

Life teaches us who we want to be and who we'll become. We must decide what we fill ourselves up with along the way—meaning, what our soul collects, our heart projects.

I started feeling my capacity up with alcohol back in my early twenties. I could drink a whole bottle to myself easily at any time of the day. I never admitted that I was an alcoholic back then, but I was. I just didn't see it that way because I never truly stopped to see the effects it had on me. I just saw it as an outlet, an escape to relieve and release my demons for a few hours, not actually fathoming that I was only creating more along the way. I used alcohol to cure almost every situation I faced: bad day at work, argument with friends or family, celebrations and sufferings. It became a natural responsive habit to any affliction I faced. At first it was only a social activity for me, never seeing the change in tide go from a social activity to a dependency issue.

Alcohol helped subdue my mind. It was my trick to dealing with my emotional instability, as well as my inability to confess my pain. But the alcohol was doing more than just fortifying my pain and trauma. It was forging my anger in a fire I didn't see growing inside of me. When we're not aware of what's growing inside of us, we can tend to make decisions from hidden places. Our minds and bodies can act out on our hidden pain, our ignored trauma, our caged voices, and our silent cries. This is what alcohol did for me.

It was a sunny summer day in July. I was out at my parents' house, working on my car. I was doing a simple brake job and planned on washing my car before I head out to enjoy the day with a girl I was dating at the time named Juana. Keep in mind, it was around 12:00 p.m. when I started working on the car. I ended up finishing up around 2:00 p.m. I headed home afterward to wash up, change, and get ready for a fun day in the sun. It didn't go as planned though. I ended up getting into a huge blowup with Juana. She was upset at me that it took so long to finish up with my car, also that I wasn't answering my phone. It blew to the point where Juana ended up leaving the house to go and hang out with friends. Well this left me with a few options, but I picked the first option right away: to have a drink. That's how it always started for me: a simple drink. I ran to the liquor store to get a bottle of Southern Comfort. Yes, I consumed that back then. My friends and family used to heckle me about drinking Southern Comfort because of the harsh taste it leaves, but it did the trick for me in terms of getting a quick buzz.

As I began drinking, one drink led to another drink, which led me to drinking the whole bottle by myself at the house. It was around 7:00 or 8:00 p.m. when I finished the bottle, I believe, and I decided to go out for a drink at the local bar that I frequented. I drove there of course. Back then I never told myself that I was drunk. I always made the excuse that I was a little buzz but never drunk. I made it to the bar safely and quickly, ended up staying there until about 11:00 p.m. I can't recall how much I had to drink, but I do remember partying with a group of people and having an array of different liquors: vodka, tequila, and whiskey, not to mentioned, I had already devoured that whole bottle of Southern Comfort before I arrived.

I eventually left. But I knew at that point, I was a little too tipsy to drive home, plus I didn't want to see my girlfriend at the house while I was drunk. So I decided my friend's house was closer of a drive for me. So that was what I did. I drove to my friend's house and just happen to catch my friend and his wife leaving to go out for the night. My friend helped me into his house and laid me on the couch, and I did what any drunk person would do: fell asleep right away. That was until my sleep was rudely interrupted by the police. Yes, the cops came into my friend's house, grabbed me off the couch, and proceeded to arrest me. At the time, I had no clue as to why. But I soon found out. Apparently while I was on my way to the friend's house, I drove my car through the front lawn of my friends' neighbor's and decimated their white picket fence and ran over their mailbox. Somehow I did all that but managed to park my car perfectly between two trees that towered in my friend's front yard. I went to jail that night. I was booked and later charged with a DUI. This wouldn't be my only drunken mistake. Over the years I would have many—from passing out at friend's house, trying to fight off four cops from arresting me inside my parents' house, car accidents, and many more.

I had filled my capacity with alcohol, and my reasoning became an inability to use sound judgments and make reasonable decisions about my life. This was what happened when my capacity had been contaminated. It was never clear to me that what I portrayed outwardly was directly linked to my capacity inwardly. This was what I was failing to recognize within myself, but alcohol wouldn't be my only damnation.

Drugs

I wish I was never exposed to drugs. I've seen friends die over what some people call recreational activity. But I don't see anything recreational about it when lying dead in an open coffin. Luckily my sin to drugs wasn't because I was consuming the product, it was because I was selling the inventory of demand: cocaine. If there was anything I hated more, it was drugs. I had been around it most of the earlier years of my life. But at that time, it was merely weed and popping pills, never saw coke really until I got in the nightlife. If you'll remember what I said earlier in that chapter, that lifestyle gives way to exposure, escape, and excess. Cocaine gave people that sensation. Back then I wasn't selling Christ, I was selling coke. So how'd it all start? In jail.

I was about twenty-five years of age around this time, I was in jail on thirty days of work release. I was sentenced to the work release program over an assault charge at a nightclub I received a few months prior, another night of what happens when I consumed entirely too much alcohol. The work release program is an option that can be given to individuals that have small amount of time to serve, individuals that are gainfully employed, and those that are at low risk of repeating criminal behavior. The idea is that a person can be released from jail up to six days per week for up to twelve hours a day to perform their job and return to jail. It was no fun driving myself to jail every day, but it was better than being in jail all day every day. The crazy thing about it was that I had a night job during this time but didn't want to let my employer know that I had gotten into trouble and that I was going to have to spend time in jail. Remember how I said in the early chapter that I knew most of the owners in the city that had restaurants and nightclubs that I would frequent? Well I ended up asking one of the owners to sign off on my work release paperwork. So when I would get out of jail each day at around 7:00 p.m., I would go to work for a few hours at night. But once I was done with work, I would stop at the house, change clothes, and head to the bars or clubs. I'd stay out until closing then head home around 4:00 or 5:00 a.m. to shower, shave, and change clothes then head back to jail and sleep through the day and do it all over again at 7:00 p.m. It wasn't really jail. It seemed more like an overnight stay at a rundown motel.

It was here that I would meet my cellmate Tommy. Tommy and I had realized that we knew most of the same people in our city, given both our track records for being out in the social nightlife. We just had never met each other personally before. Tommy had the same schedule as I did. And because he was in the nightlife scene as well, he'd do the same as I did. We became friends instantly, given our obsession for the same social propensities. We must be careful of the people that randomly get placed in our lives. It could be a setup for opportunity or trap toward a downfall. Keep in mind, I was in parallel, still trying to validate my sense of self.

Tommy invited me to meet up with him on one of the nights we were on work release, which I did. It became a world that I knew about but stayed out of for so long. But I quickly was connected. I met tons of people and had even more exposure to the behind-the-scenes nightlife that I never had before. With that exposure came more girls, alcohol, and of course drugs—lots of drugs. That was all Tommy and his friends did: sold drugs. But looking at them from the onset, I'd never know it because it wasn't about drugs for them. Drugs for them was just a part of their everyday life. What they cared about more was family, community, and connections. We were a quiet city mob back then. Most people would have never known we were selling drugs. We were connected with everyone: owners, staff, security. Heck, we even hung out with athletes, reporters, and cops. We did meals together, spend time with each other's families, and even hang out on the holidays. On Thanksgiving, we started a tradition to feed the homeless. We'd use one of the nightclubs to cook, host, and feed the homeless. It truly felt like a family. And for some reason, for the first time in my life, I felt like I belonged, but quietly I was still lost. At first I was only around them to hang out and have a good time. I never thought of getting into drugs. For one reason, I never needed to. I didn't do drugs, and I had a good paying job, so I didn't need the money either. But like one youth pastor of mine once said, "Show me your friends, and I'll show you you're future," never thinking that it would refer to me someday. I'd eventually started selling drugs, mostly because people always assumed I had drugs because of who I was connected with, so in my mind, it just made sense to carry cocaine on me. It was a stupid reason, I know but remember what I said about my capacity being contaminated as well as the broken pieces I already shared.

I was selling cocaine in hotels, to partygoers, in the bar, in the nightclubs, to DJs, friends, and security, at after-parties, as well as owners and other people that came around. Then I would go to work the next day like a normal person. I was in a season where I was living in two worlds. One world was the nightlife and all the surrounding activities that came with it then my normal world where I would hang out with my family, go to work, hit the gym, and relax at home, never cross-pollinating either two worlds. I was two different people, and nobody knew. The people in the nightlife didn't know my day life and vice versa. I was a chameleon.

I stayed connected and associated to drug scene for many years. Tommy and I eventually had a falling out to the point that on one night, we pulled our guns out on each other over a silly dispute. It was eventually calmed down by friends, but our relationship was never the same after that. We'd see each other around and always showed love, but it was different now, especially because I was still connected, and Tommy went on his own. Tommy even tried to warn me to walk away from those people, but I didn't listen. It was what created our tension in the first place. Sometimes life will send pre-warnings before the warning. We mustn't miss the signs. I did.

Everything for me came to a screeching halt one night. I had gotten into a fight at one of the clubs we moved drugs out of. It was pretty bad. I put a guy's head through glass because I lost my patience with him all because the individual got too drunk, and I asked him to leave the establishment. And when the individual refused, I roughed him up, not realizing the cops where right outside. The owner told me to take off because the cops were going to come, given all the hostile commotion that was happening. But as I was leaving, people started pointing me out. The cops saw me and asked me to stop. But in my panic, I took off and started running.

When I would watch the show *Cops* on TV, I never understood how people couldn't outrun cops. I always told myself, "If that was me, I would surely outrun a few cops, given my speed." For the most part, I did until a few cops showed up on bikes. But as soon as I cut into an alley to continue to get away from the cops, surprisingly one of my friends had grabbed the car to come save me. I have no clue how my friend even found me. I swear I felt like I was in a movie. I hopped in his car, and we sped off. But as we drove out the alley, more cops were there to cut us off. My friend almost hit the cops as we cruised around them off onto another street. Now my simple assault has turned into a high-speed chase through the city streets on a busy Friday night. There were at least eight cop cars chasing us. We eventually got cornered and ran off the road. Cops all around us ran up on our vehicle, guns drawn, telling us to put our hands up and step out of the vehicle. It's crazy to think how I survived that night.

I could have been killed that night, but never once did it cross my mind. The cops arrested us both. And off to jail, we went. That wasn't even the worst part. It so happened that my friend's car was filled with cocaine, money, and guns, all of which I became tied to. As I sat in jail, yet again my mind did what I almost always seemed to do, I tried to ascertain how I could allow my life to have gotten this bad. I was meant for more, but my circumstances were often telling me different. Eventually all the charges against me would be dropped. My friend took the responsibility for the whole thing, plus the feds were already after him for other drug-related crimes that I had no clue about. Additionally, the guy I assaulted that night never filed charges. It was as if the event never took place, but it did. It was my warning to get out, and that was exactly what I ended up doing. I stopped selling drugs and got out of that circle, the same circle Tommy told me to get away from a year earlier, because it was becoming too hot. But I was so lost in my own need to be a part of something, not realizing that I was risking losing my entire life.

Violence

So what is violence? Well by definition, violence "is the behavior involving to hurt, damage, or kill someone or something." Another reads, "strength of emotion or unpleasant or destructive natural force." It sounds pretty serious stuff to say the least. Unfortunately, violence in the world is becoming all too common. In fact it's safe to say we're seeing all sorts of violence play out all around us every day in our own society, communities, and local environments. News outlets, media companies, social media forums, news feeds and more seduce and enthrall us with these fearful and distributing tales every day. As the viewer we say to ourselves, "these people are crazy," or "what were they thinking?" It's always easier to reach toward a judgmental perspective from the sidelines, but I'd further the questioning a little deeper. Understand, violence is merely the result of an action taken from a choice decided based on an individual's capacity to feel and reason. It's not merely whether individuals acting out are crazy or not, it's about understanding the capacity within ourselves to make reasonable choices. It's about understanding the intentionality of the individual. Also we must ask ourselves, if we all have the capacity for emotion and reasoning, what are we filling our capacity with, and how can we be aware of its effecting nature on our lives, both inwardly and outwardly? If my anger was going to continue to fill my capacity, I would never have a chance.

> This is a very violent place to live, the earth,
> and we're a very violent species. Cain is still kill-
> ing Abel. We see it every day. (Anne Lamott)

As I pointed the gun at his face and aimed, I had a moment before I pulled the trigger. Life is about moments. This was one of my biggest moments. There was one time after a night out that I had gotten into an altercation with someone I didn't care too much about. It's important to note that this person never did anything to me directly. In fact every time this guy came around me, he showed nothing but love and respect because he knew I was connected. But something about him just got under my skin, and back then it didn't take much. This night, however, it would come out.

This guy owned a party bus and would often be around town lighting up the city with fun and exciting bus parties, everyone knew him. Often after a night out, he would grab whoever wanted to party longer into the night and allow them to come on the bus and hang out. One night he grabbed a few people that where friends of mine, one person happened to be my ex-girlfriend, and took them out for a ride so they could continue to party. Later when my friends decided they wanted to leave the bus, they were told they couldn't. My friends were stuck and felt trapped. My ex-girlfriend, who was on the bus, called me to tell me what was happening and where they were at, and I was there in minutes. During this time of my life, it was dark and cloudy often. As I arrived, I remember my blood boiling over. I grabbed a gun from my glove box and hopped out the car. I got on the bus and immediately told my friends to get out and told the guy to follow as well. This guy wasn't alone though and had his friends with him, but I didn't really ever pay it no mind. Back then I was careless and unafraid, ignorant as well. I asked the guy to explain why he had my friends stuck on the bus, but the guy kept denying the fact, which only set me off even more. Furious and tired of the lies I felt were being told, I took the gun and held it point blank at the guy's face, demanding for him to tell me the truth. All of my friends were yelling and pleading with me to stop and let it go, but it got quiet. I couldn't hear anything. I only saw the moment I was in. I saw the future that I would lose if I pulled the trigger. I saw the kid that I was supposed to become, not the person I became. I decided to pull the trigger anyway, but not at his face, instead I shot off around into the air and gave the guy a warning and left the scene immediately with my friends. I made a choice in the moment but didn't see the opportunity of the long-term redirect. I knew I needed to change my life, but I didn't know how. I was starting to realize that my life was being guided by one emotion, my capacity was filled with anger.

What do we do when all we know is anger? Where do we go when we don't know how to ask for help? What becomes of us if who we really want to be or need to be is locked up and dormant? Does all this excuse my actions? No, not it all. But it does provide the underlining narrative and the transparency of my capacity. You see, earlier when I said that I never had a chance, I was speaking to the fact that because of my untreated trauma as a child, it limited my capacity for reasoning and emotion later on in my adult life. We can't simply tag a label to something without first understanding what it is that it represents. Was I a criminal who committed violent and wrongful acts? Yes. But remember, violence is the result of a choice, a choice determined by my capacity to reason and feel, both inwardly and outwardly. It's important to understand the root of the tree before we label the fruit of it.

The Broken Piece: Anger

Where there is anger, there is always pain underneath

—Eckhart Tolle

So I must begin to ask myself and uncover the mystery that lives within me. What is my anger masking inside of me that is dying to come out and speak? Anger, by definition, "is a strong feeling of being upset or annoyed because of something wrong or bad, the feeling that makes someone want to hurt other people; to shout." For me, I've often been criticized for my actions and behaviors while people rarely ever consider my pain. The problem with me was that anger became my voice, my reasoning, and more so my shield to protect myself from the continuing conflict of my pain and fear. If we never have empathy for people's anger, we'll never give a voice to the pain and fear. I needed to find my voice for my pain and fear. I needed mercy to come out and know that I was safe. I needed grace to be accepted and know I was not alone. I needed healing to be free and no longer captive to my pain or fear. And I needed people to see and recognize I was broken so that I could smile again. The problem was no one did, and I never told them. So my anger continued to grow and fuel my outward perspective.

I often would have moments during my twenties where I couldn't believe who I'd became. Furthermore I despised myself for the things I'd done and the people that I affected along the way. I made up my own image of who I was and what I wanted others to see. And in doing so, lost myself and who I was always meant to become. I ran away from my family, upbringing, and purpose and traded it in for a secondary life in the streets that no one close to me even knew about. I had hidden trauma that was quietly lurking, taking root in my life, and was developing branches that would spawn fruits of violence and pain for those that came around me.

Those that knew me only saw what I wanted them to see because deep down inside I was hiding my pain and my mess. And instead of living out my reality, treating my wounds, and accepting myself, I clothed myself in what I thought others would accept or fear. I was dying on the inside and outside, and no one knew. Worse of all, I didn't know how to see it. My capacity had shrunken down to the level of my perspective of myself. I was reaching a point of my life where there was no return if I didn't course correct. I knew that my life would only be shorten. I would spend many more nights behind closed cells in orange jumpsuits, continuing to throw more of my life away, wrapping myself in more anger and even deeper shame.

CHAPTER 8

Jail

Guilt says, "You failed." Shame says, "You're a failure."
Grace says, "Your failures are forgiven."

—Lecrae

I lost my freedom once before; I couldn't believe I had now lost it
again. At that moment, I looked back at the last decade of my life
and the experiences that led me down this path. For most that knew
me never knew of my secret prisons.

Reality

As I awoke to the brown, thin linen blanket wrapped around
my body, barely covering me from head to toe, lying there on the thin
cracked, stained mattress that separated me from the metal-mounted
bed frame. I began to ask myself "where am I?"

Rising from the discomfort of my bed bunk to the noise of loud
banter, I sat on the edge of the bed. My body immediately startled as
my feet hit the cold pavement of the cement floor. Taking a glance at
my surroundings, I noticed a small draped vanilla cotton curtain that

hid the grotesque amenity of a communal lavatory, the thin curtain being the only thing to separate it from the main recreation room. But it didn't do the same for the stench. As I continued to observe, I saw men gathered around in various areas; some were sitting around at tables, playing card games, telling stories, or repulsive jokes; other men were sitting on bed bunks, either watching the time go by, reading books, or staring off into their own stream of consciousness; while some men were yelling to one another from across the room. A few guys gathered around the small mounted TV in the corner of the room, watching the latest news broadcast; and every so often, there would be someone on the pay phone in the distant corner, speaking to someone who I could only assume to be a loved one.

As I continued to look around, I noticed a small crinkled brown paper bag at the corner of my bed. In the bag, I found toiletries and food items, such as a toothbrush, toothpaste, bar of soap, bologna sandwich, bag of crackers, and a packet of grape flavored juice powder. As I fumbled through the items of the bag, others took notice and ask if I was willing to part with certain items, the vultures came running. I grunted with an authoritative *no*. It became clear that my items where not up for sell or bargaining. As I continued to contemplate the reality of my situation, a loud yell came through the microphone speaker, saying, "Section B, line up for chow." I noticed as everyone got into a single-file line, remembering back to my preschool days when teachers would have us kids line up before going outside to play. But this wasn't that kind of playground. I looked down and put on my rubber-made orange sandals and got in line. As the loud doors would begin to slowly open, a female voice could be heard saying, "Come out and stay in a single-file line. When I call your name, come get your chow and head back in." While I was standing in line, I observed how others seemed to have an extreme ease of comfort and inherit acclimatization to these procedures. When my name got called, "William McGee!" they yelled. I quickly followed as others did, grabbed my food, glanced at the portions, and began to antiquate the smell and suspected taste, while deliberating on what I would actually consume.

As I headed back in to the white-painted walls of the cement room of my environment, I sat at the table with others, listening to the instant banter about the food and the quick exchange of agreements being made. It was like being on the trading room floor of the stock exchange. "I'll give you my fruit for your bread," or "remember when I traded you my juice packet. You owe me some of your spaghetti." Often someone would ask me if I was going to eat all my food or to notify them if I didn't want something on my plate. The vultures were back again but this time with more persistence. I ate all that seemed to be the most nutritional or desirable to my taste buds and handed over the rest of it to whoever was the closest to me. I made my way back to my bunk. As I sat there, I glanced out, observing the dialog, tendencies, and personalities of each individual come out in various ways. I quickly made my assertions and assumptions about who was who and what their story may be. Very few people talked to me, not because they didn't want to or because I told them not too but more so because I naturally had a very intimidating personality, or at least that's what I've always been told. A few men would approach me to make small talk and get a better understanding of my story, often wondering what my workout routine was for how I garnered my muscles. My response was always the same, "Eat a lot and be consistent. It comes over time, not overnight." For the most part, I kept to myself, not because I saw myself better than others or that I didn't like people, but simply because I didn't plan on making this place my home like many others that were in there had already seemed to do. I wasn't there to make friends. I knew that this wasn't where I belonged.

As I laid back down on my bunk, covering myself with the small blanket, the reality of my environment and situation begin to set in. I couldn't sleep at all; my mind wondered the edges of my entire life, replaying over and over again all the decisions made throughout my life to that point. Questions surmounted the abyss of my soul. "What happen?" "Where did I go wrong?" "How did I get offtrack?" I thought I was meant for more than this. It finally hit me. I was back in a place of isolation. I was back in place that my story had started. This time the environment was different. I realized I was in jail.

Secrets

Getting into trouble was never on the agenda of my road map. In fact I was a bright, intelligent kid who could have made anything with my life. But sometimes the model that we need to follow that guides and gives us direction as an adolescent gets ignored. Sometimes if left to our own devices, the environments we put ourselves in often become the catalyst that cultivates our character. This happens to be true of me. I would find my first run-in with the law during my early twenties, about the time I would turn twenty-one actually. During this time, I would often visit a local restaurant to eat breakfast or lunch with my friends and family. It was located on a busy freeway, next to a frequently visited mall. Sometimes I would go there on late nights after work. On one night, I observed people coming in and out of the back part of the restaurant, younger people around my age, and even a few older adults. It seemed like a bar or lounge from my observations. I didn't think much of it though, after all that wasn't my scene at the time, but I did take notice. The more I visited the restaurant, the more I realized that it was an after-hours bar where individuals would go hang out to drink and socialize after their meal, or some would come in just to go hang out in the back, never eating dinner at all. I didn't drink, listen to loud music, or party all that much around this time of my life, so I would just eat my food and simply continue on my way. It did start to intrigue me though, wondering what all the fun was about. I had a girlfriend that lived right up the road from the restaurant that I would often visit before or after work. Sometimes I would even stay the night.

On one night after work, I had gotten into a heated argument with my girlfriend and decided to leave her house and blow off some stem. I found myself walking down the street late at night, figuring out what to do and how to calm down. I decided to visit the local restaurant, seeing how it was right down the hill from my girlfriend's house. As I walked through the door, I could hear the music and joyful vibes coming from the back. I only intended to grab a quick bite and cool down then head back up the hill to settle the argument, but that never happened. Quickly I found myself in the back of the restaurant—the place that I never visited, only always imagined what it must have looked like all those times while I was eating dinner. It wasn't a big area at all but enough to fit about twenty-five to thirty people in there if it wanted to, but it never got that busy. The crowd was lively, and everyone seemed to be having a good time. I quickly forgot about the fight with my girlfriend and immediately knew that I wanted to have fun, enjoy the scene with others, and ignore my problems. I made my way to the bar, not ever having ordered a drink or sat at a bar before, looking at all the bottles to figure out what sounded good enough to drink. I saw a bottle labeled "Southern Comfort" and was immediately sold on the idea of it being a comfortable drink. I guess branding does work sometimes. I placed my drink order with the bartender but was quickly convinced to order a double instead for an extra two dollars, which I ended up agreeing too. As I stood there waiting for my drink, I began to observe my surroundings, looking on at the people dancing to the music; groups of people standing around the tables, chatting it up; others playing pool or darts; and few people at the bar sitting there, watching TV. For me it felt like something I had been missing out on this whole time.

At that point of my life, all I knew growing up was sports, church, family, and work. The bars and drinking were never something that appealed to me. I saw it in my family of course, but I always knew that I didn't want to indulge in that lifestyle. We must be watchful when our circumstances begin to change our inhibitions. As I began to walk around and check out the scene further, I met a group of people sitting by the pool table. I was very personable and made friends easily, so it wasn't hard for me to quickly fit in and connect with others. The group I met happened to be regulars of the bar and seemed to know just about everyone, which I would soon meet myself. I had a good time that night, conversing, drinking, laughing, joking, and even playing a few rounds of pool. I don't think I ever did go back to address that argument with my girlfriend. The bar would become an often scene for me on the weekends especially, and soon I would be known as a regular myself. This is where my indulgence for alcohol and nightlife was quietly birthed.

On one weekend I was in there, the regular bartender that I was accustomed to ordering from and that knew everyone's drink by heart was out on vacation. This new bartender didn't like me, and it was obvious to tell, often not even listening to my drink orders or never showing up with the drink even after it was ordered. I tried to ignore it the best I could, but after a few drinks in and mistakes continuing to be made, it really began to get under my skin. I addressed the bartender about it, but it quickly turned into a loud argument, which eventually others in the bar would jump in and break up, but I was still frustrated about it.

The following week, I decided to go to the local restaurant during the day when it wasn't busy and have a few drinks and play some pool with a friend. The same bartender was there that I had a dispute with the prior weekend, but I didn't pay it no attention. I went to the bar, ordered my drinks, and went to the pool tables to begin playing a round. As my friend and I continued to play the pool game, I realized that the drinks hadn't shown up yet. Once again, I became furious as this only reminded me of what took place the prior weekend. Curious as to why, I decided to go to the bar and figure it out. As I approached the bar, I calmly asked the bartender, as not to insight another argument, where the drinks were at that I ordered a while ago and communicated that I hadn't receive them yet. The bartender went on to inform me that he was no longer serving me any drinks. I was quickly confused as to why, being that my friend and I had only been there for roughly fifteen minutes. I asked the bartender why wasn't he serving me any drinks. The bartender told me simply because he didn't want to and that he had the right to refuse service to anyone he wanted to. This obviously didn't sit well with me. With now even more confusion on my face and deepening frustration setting in, I asked again, "Why are you not serving me drinks, and what did I do that would make you not serve me?" Again the bartender repeated himself, telling me that he refused to serve me. At that point, my blood was starting to boil over, and my pride was setting in. Now instead of asking for a drink, I was demanding the bartender to pour me a drink because I didn't believe I was in the wrong. At that point, the bartender was getting upset himself, even cursing back at me and telling me that I needed to leave. My friend could tell that the situation was starting to go south and grabbed me, trying to encourage me to leave and go somewhere else. But it was too late, my pride and anger superseded my ability to reason. The frontal lobe of my brain had shut down and went for a coffee break.

The bartender and I kept going back and forth as onlookers began to take notice at the heated debate. Even some staff from the restaurant begin to trickle in to the back of the bar area. The emotion just continued to elevate within the room, neither person backing down. As the arguing continued, the bartender began threatening to remove me physically if I didn't leave, but I wasn't backing down at all. I was already too emotionally invested. I began challenging the bartender to come around the bar and remove me himself. As the bartender proceeded to come from around the bar, I was quick to meet him with a hard push to the chest, which caused the bartender to fly back. As the bartender was flying back, I was on the attack, hitting him with several punches to the face and body. The fight spilled all through the back of the bar while others tried to break it apart. It became impossible to wrestle apart me and the bartender. The fight eventually made its way out from behind the bar and onto the main floor of the bar area. At that point, I picked up the bartender and slammed him to the ground. And as I attempted to jump on the bartender and keep inflicting pain, others were able to grab me and pull me off the bartender. I soon rushed out of the restaurant where my friend advised me to get in the car and leave before the cops got to the scene. I did just that, and we drove away.

Soon after I was down the street at the mall parking lot, trying to calm down and put together everything that had just transpired as the adrenaline continued to perforate throughout my body. I soon realized that through all the scuffle and hustle of getting out of there, I'd lost my phone. It wasn't too long after that I had found out that the cops had it, and they were looking for me. I decided to turn myself in as I sure didn't want to be the next person seen on an episode of *Cops*. After all it was the first time I had ever faced any real trouble with the law outside of being caught shoplifting as a little kid, but my parents made me pay the price for that. But it wouldn't be the last time either. Over the course of my life, I would be arrested and in jail for multiple offenses, assaults, DUIs, drug possession, evading the cops, hit and run, and other transgressions, never seeing that the course of that one event and argument with my girlfriend that night set off a chain reaction of events that led me back behind bars at the age of thirty-four.

In all of these events through the course of my life, most of my family and closest friends never knew. People close to me never knew the countless times I had been in jail or gotten into trouble. They couldn't tell. For the most part, everything else around my life was normal. I went to work, paid my bills, hang out with friends and family, went to church even, but no one really knew that I was out late most nights drinking and often getting into some kind of trouble. Not to mention, I had a short fuse and a lot of anger. Who I was and what people saw were two totally different things. I didn't want people to see my stains, only my polish. I never wanted people to see what I was truly doing, because for the most part, it was never what I intended my life to be.

My shame quickly overtook my ability to see myself. My shame began to block my purview of my value. My shame forced me into the false reality that who I was wasn't enough, that I had to transform into what others wanted to believe about me. I lost myself in my shame. My biggest secret was myself. I had hidden it so that I could live among others, with them never knowing what or who I truly was—a flawed person. Sometimes if we're not careful, we can fall into the lies or misconceptions of what we tell ourselves about ourselves. Sometimes if we stand still for too long looking at our flaws, we'll only see our inabilities instead of our potential capabilities. Though I always knew I was meant for more, my life often never painted that picture. The painting on my walls wasn't one to be admired or appreciated. To me it was one that was abhorrent and unpleasant. The personal conflicts in our lives can often lead us to inducing ourselves temporarily or sometimes even permanently with a negative ideology of who we are or can be. If we're not careful, our souls lose out when our shame remains present. My heart no longer lived, breathed, or walked in freedom but in the bondage and captivity of my predispositions. So because I went untreated, the shame became the malignant fate of my heart. We need to be careful when sitting in the courtroom of our hearts and minds not to sentence ourselves to a lifetime of shame.

Courtroom

There's an old proverb that says, "In the courtroom of the conscience, a case is always in progress." For those that have been to a courtroom via personal issues or serving jury duty or even watched a courtroom drama on television, it's clear to see that it's an environment of justice, judgment, jurors, and judges. The justice system holds up the law against those that break it. Judgment is the pronouncements placed against a defendant that's been charged with breaking such law. Jurors listen and discuss the facts of the case and give an unbiased opinion on the judgment, and the judges define the final ruling, verdict, or sentencing of judgment against said defendant.

This happens every day in our country on many different levels. This allows us as a people to serve and uphold the justice and the rights of our laws and constitutions against those that break it. But I don't want to spend time breaking down the judicial systems and processes here. I want to spend time discussing the courtroom that was going on in my soul. If we're not cognizant of how we operate as people, we may very well be serving our own brand of justice unjustly in our own lives. Welcome to the courtroom of my conscience. I was prolonging the persecution of myself and sending my soul to a lifetime of prison in my own courtroom. Allow me to explain.

The justice of my soul were the values I chose in my life to uphold. These were my core beliefs about myself and how I saw the world around me. My value system was broken. I cared about money, power, and respect and traded my soul for such. The judgments I passed down were the assessments I made about myself. These are often based on the situations I've been placed in, whether good or bad, intentional or unintentional. What I said about myself after my failure and trauma was broken. The jurors are the voices around me—social media, society, friends, family—that make their opinions about me based on what they may or may not know and often declare an unbiased or sometimes biased decision about who I was. The voices I allowed into my life were broken. The judge, well that was me—I was the one that was often sending my soul to prison. I was so broken that all I was left with was my shame.

My point here is simply this: I wasn't a perfect person. No matter how strong the morals, traditions, and somewhat good values that I held too, from time to time, I broke them. I went against them. I failed many of times. I made many mistakes. And I hurt people along the way. What I want you to see here is that more than often, what I said about myself carried more weight than the actual failure made and the trauma I endured. Sometimes we allow the jurors of our lives to influence the judgments about ourselves, often compromising our own internal justices and passing down a false verdict of lifelong guiltiness. That was what I had done for many years. I sat in shame and condemnation.

The Broken Piece: Shame

Guilt says, "You failed." Shame says, "You're a failure."
Grace says, "Your failures are forgiven."

—Lecrae

Most people didn't know me because I was locked up in prison most of my life. I don't mean a real prison, I mean the prison of my soul. By definition, shame is "a painful feeling of humiliation or distress caused by the consciousness of wrong or foolish behavior." You see, because I faced trauma and made failures throughout my life, my shame of not becoming kept me from becoming who I was destined to be.

For me, it was my alcohol addiction, selling drugs, the nightclubs, violence, and the shame allowing those to take root in my life.

I never lived free. I was constantly living in a state of captivity over my past. Every time I sat in jail, it only reminded me of how much I failed. For me, my prison was the shame that had formed through-out my life, furthermore the fear of others finding out who or what I truly was about. I'd made mistakes throughout my life, often hurting the very ones I was supposed to love and protect, but I was flawed and didn't want others to see it.

My anger and shame eventually led me down a path of desola-tion. I could no longer tell good from bad or right from left. I was lost. I didn't know how to get back to who I was meant to be. I was stuck in a wilderness of broken pieces.

CHAPTER 9

Wilderness

Many of us crucify ourselves between two thieves—
regret for the past and fear of the future.

—Fulton Oursler

I never knew I was lost until I needed to be found. Who knew that it would come through a phone call? I was twenty-eight years of age at the time. And up until then, my life had a lot of moments but lacked any real meaning. The thickets of my condition and reality continued to tell me the same narrative as my earlier years that I was alone with no identity and no purpose. I was a man that could only see my life through the shame and regret of my history. I truly felt that this was the last chapter of my story.

Culmination

My twenties were some rough years for me. On the outside, no one could see that though. I had a successful career. I was at the gym working out every day, and my body was in shape. I constantly had a good-looking girl in my arm. I was out every night partying and drinking the night away. I had tons of friends. And on top of all that, I had plenty of money in the bank. My life would seem good to the observer, to the discerner it was not. My exterior looked amazing, but my interior was destitute. I had spent so many years making my name great and doing everything I could to appeal to what I thought society wanted me to be and who I felt I needed to be but along the way lost who I was created to be: myself. The hardest part was that I could feel it but lacked the capacity to change it. My broken pieces had caught up with me, but I wasn't ready to confront it. Honestly, I didn't know how to. And, furthermore, who would accept my truth? After all everyone knew Antonious, nobody ever knew Will.

Antonious

It's almost nearly impossible to get lost physically nowadays with the help of technology and the ability to have a phone to be a 24-7 guide. I rarely find myself in that predicament. But what happens when we get off course with our lives when we need to be rerouted? There is a moment in everyone's life where we get offtrack, not just directionally but personally, whether it's in business, family, finances, personal lives, or the family road trips. Unfortunately at times, we go down the wrong path. That's life. It will happen even to the best of us. Nobody heads down one path or the same path forever. Sometimes it's the detours of life that allows us to find the meaning of our lives, to find ourselves. But there are also times that if we stay too long on the misguided path, we'll lose our way; we'll lose our lives.

To this day, my mom doesn't even allow the name Antonious to come out in her presence. She hates it that much. Just the mere mention of Antonious brings a negative connotation to the environment, not just for my mom either but for most people that knew me by this name as well. My mom will tell you that when I started going by that name was the same time she felt that she had lost me. I understand because it was a name my mother never gave me, but it would be the name that I would use to make myself known. In my mind, the name

Will or William brought back all those emotions and images of my childhood and early years that I wanted to leave behind. Antonious almost became an alternate reality for me, if that makes any sense. Will was soft, kind, generous, empathic, quiet, thoughtful, vulnerable, and loving. Antonious was hard, angry, prideful, egotistical, narcissistic, impatient, disrespectful, and heartless. Antonious protected William. Antonious was like the nineties version of DMX. I just didn't care about myself or who I'd have to hurt along the way.

Coming out of my adolescent years and heading into the early stages of being an adult, that new name and moment came on my twenty-first birthday. Around this time, coming out of my school days, struggling to define my identity while fraught with the stress of what I was going to do in life, I became susceptible to others defining it for me. Unfortunately, I wasn't cautious about how I lived my life then, therefore I'd miss moments that came to determine my life, moments that decided the man I was to become. It started with a name, then it would plunge into a lifestyle until the age of twenty-one, I always went by the name my momma gave me. But around this time, I chose to go by something different, something that would become more than just a name. We must be careful to know who we are. If we don't stand for who we're meant to be, we'll let the world decide who we're going to be. For me, William was no longer. He was dead to me. I became Antonious.

By the time I turned twenty-one, I'd already been exposed to many realities of what life could offer me, of what life I could choose to live. I saw examples of education, hard work, alcohol, drug dealing, church, abuse, arguing, anger, military, success, and much more in and around my household.

There was one time when I was about fifteen years of age, and I was hanging out over at my brother's house, playing video games as I did often. My brother told me that he needed to run an errand and that he wanted me to go with him. At the time, I wasn't sure what the errand was or where we were going. But I decided to go with him anyway. It was late at night, and not much was open. And as we were driving, I could tell that it was something serious as it was quite clear from the demeanor of my brother's face during the drive.

As we approached an apartment complex, my brother began to turn down his music as not to set off any car alarms or draw attention to his own vehicle. Once parked, I sat there for a minute, looking around at the environment, trying to configure in my mind what this could all be about. As I surveyed the scene, I watched my brother prepare something in his lap and rolled it up in a brown paper bag. Oblivious to what it could possibly be at the time, I continued to sit there and wait for my brother to run his errand or at least tell me why we were even there in the first place. A few minutes now passed, and I heard my brother say, "Listen up, this is what I want you to do. Take this bag and go to apartment number 1267. Knock on the door. Someone will come to the door. When they open the door, don't say anything. Hand them the bag. Once you do, they'll hand you the money. Don't come back to the car without the money. Go straight there, and come straight back. Don't talk to anyone, and don't look in the bag. You'll be okay. I'll be here watching the whole time."

After hearing this, I was both scared and confused. After all I just came over to play some video games, not be part of a drug exchange. But I didn't know it was drugs at the time. Reluctantly, I decided to do it. I was scared the whole time, not sure what was going to leap out at me in the night. It was a windy and cold night at that, and I was in the middle of nowhere in some run-down, beaten-up apartments, running an errand I never signed up for. It wasn't the moment, but it was a moment that never left me. Sometimes the little subtle experiences that our lives get exposed to can be foreshadowings of what we become accustom to, whether we know it or not. Once I made it back to the car and of course with the money, I was upset. I was angry. I didn't quite know why at the time. Thinking back on it now, I believe it was the fear of being exposed to something that I wasn't prepared to face.

Hanging at my brother's house though, I'd always see stuff like this: drugs, guns, alcohol, followed with loud music. But I always made a choice to ignore it and just play video games. I paid it no mind. Even when my brother would try to encourage me or entice me, I'd always decline. I knew something deep in my spirit didn't want to live in that reality, but I never realized that the exposure would be the subtle sarcoma that would take root in my life through the connection with my brother. Sometimes what we're connected to can be the life source in which the fabric of our life contours to. We need to be careful of who we're connected to, whether by blood or relationship. If we're not wise to it, the composition of our character can be formed by those around us.

Growing up, I knew the truth of what my life was supposed to be, but I wasn't connected to it, if that makes sense. We can live in a moment or reality and never be connected to it. This happens in households today: fathers that are home but not present, wives that are in marriages but detached, and siblings related by blood but disengaged with love. It's the new norm of our society today. It's the reason why so many broken homes and broken people exist around the world. My moment nonetheless would come on my twenty-first birthday though. My brother would actually be the one to give me the name Antonious that day and told me that I was a man now, that I needed to take control of my own life. It was a sign that my brother wasn't going to be there no more, and I needed to fight my own battles and make my own way. I didn't know it then, but I was sitting in the middle of a moment, a moment that would decide who I would become in life, a reality that I never saw coming, and a lifestyle from which I would make my mark.

For me, it wasn't just a new name, it was a new path. No longer was I the little boy that my parents raised—not at all. I would become someone entirely different, someone people never would really ever know, only experience; someone that in time would become lost in who I became, often remembering at times the man I was supposed to become. If we don't recognize the moments in life, we can often lose our perspective on life. We must be watchful of what we expose ourselves to and the subtle natures that live in the background of them. Even though I didn't choose to follow in my brother's footsteps, I never chose not to. Understand, I grew up seeing all these things and would often tell myself that I would never go down that road, that I would never be that kind of person, that I was better than what I saw going on around me. Little did I know that there would come a time in life when my character would be tested, when my identity had to stand on trial, when my beliefs were going to be examined, and when my integrity had to make a choice. There comes a moment for us all where we must choose a path: the wilderness or the garden, life or death.

Call

See, those that knew me only knew the side I showed, so if it was work-related, then people saw the sophisticated and articulate business side of me. If it were drugs and gangbanging related, then people saw my hood degree and angry Antonious side of me. If it was church related, then people saw the holy-than-thou, man-of-God, spitting-scripture side of me. If it was gym related, then people would see the fitness side of me. But no one ever would see the true and real side of who I was. Neither did I. I had played this game for so long that I had lost my way back to me. It's often easier to appear a certain way to appeal rather than be real about who we are in fear of not fitting in or getting cancelled. It's why I fear social media is so successful today because we don't have to be real as long as we can appear a certain way to appeal to a certain audience. Unfortunately, I had been doing this in my own life for years, and it had finally loomed over my conscious and awakened every broken piece inside of me.

On one particular night, the darkness of my wilderness reached a melancholy of emotions I never knew I could get to. I was on a business trip for the week. And as was my custom after a long day of off-site meetings, I would grab a few drinks with the team or whoever I would be traveling with at the time. There was nothing special or chaotic about this night that I can recall, just a regular weekday night with a few business associates enjoying dinner and drinks. Honestly, I think my actuality had finally caught up with my reality. As I sat there watching the conversations and the laughter, I could see a projection of myself as if I had stepped outside of my body to see the whole picture of the moment I was in. On one hand, I saw everything that everyone else saw in me at that table: a confident, funny, charming, and well put-together guy. But then I could see the internal man inside of me that was often hidden away in secret, not wanting anyone to see the real me when I wasn't staging myself as the "business guy." I saw the intramural part of my being that I had become accustomed to hiding almost proficiently and skillfully in way for others to never truly know who I was. I saw the alcoholic, the guy with low self-esteem and worth. I saw the guy who had been in and out of jail and had many failed relationships with women. I saw the guy was crying inside and dying of past pain. I saw the guy who was ashamed of who he became. I saw the man that had been living dormant for years. I saw William dying.

As I sat there with the view of both the man people saw of me and the man I always hid within, a stream of despair and anger came over me. I sat there looking at the man inside of me, asking myself, "How did I get this way? Why am I so ashamed to be seen?" I immediately left dinner and went back to my room. The emotions inside of me were so heavy, I felt unequipped to carry it. No matter how much muscle mass I had obtained, it wasn't enough to hold this weight that I had stacked up over the years. As I sat there in my hotel room wrestling with myself and all the emotions, images, and flashes of everything I did in my past, everything I had become in my present, everything that I had allowed others to see, and everything that I had hidden in myself, it all came down to one distinct emotion: regret.

At that very moment sitting there in my hotel room, I had regretted my entire life. I saw nothing in my life that was worthy of accolades or recognition. My life told me I was a failure. My life told me at that moment that I was a mistake, and every regret that filled the walls of my mindset was telling me the same. I paced back and forth in my room, envisaging how the person in me could no longer contend with the man I allowed everyone to see. I had gotten to a place that I had never realized my life was heading toward. I was empty inside. Yes, I had good career, money, nice home, friends, somewhat of a family, and lot of other entities and items of value, but I never took time to value or love myself enough without all those objects in my life. Up to that point in my life, I had lived my life without any direction. I was in a wilderness the whole time and never knew. The worst part of it all was that I felt like I had no way out. I wanted to give up. I wanted to throw in the towel. I was tired and wanted out of this life. I wanted to commit suicide. I wanted to live no longer. I wanted to take the leap out of my hotel balcony. I remember saying to myself, "Would anyone care or even miss me? No one ever knew me anyways."

With my eyes and face now drowned in tears and empty sorrows and my mind buzzing from the alcohol that was starting to set in and my body shaking from the overcome of emotions, I was ready to end it all. Then my phone rang. It was my best friend at the time, Christina. I had called Christina earlier that day and forgotten all about it. She had just gotten off from work and was calling me back. Little did Christina know that she was saving my life that night. The funny thing about it was that Christina told me on the phone that she wasn't going to call me back that night because it was already so late, and she figured I wouldn't pick up. But she decided to anyways just to check in on me. That night I told Christina about my emotions and all the regret I was feeling. I never told her that I was planning to kill myself that night, a truth no one knows till this day. Not even Christina ever knew. Christina talked me through my emotions that night and encouraged me in a way that gave me hope to press on. It was my redirection. It was allowing me a detour out of my mess and out of this reality I had lived in for so long. Again I found myself in the middle of a moment. I knew that I was lost and that it was only getting darker, as was the violence.

My wilderness was one I struggled to escape, often never seeing a way out and unsure of what other life there was to live. Sometimes we're meant for more but can't see it from the enclosure of our wilderness. Sometimes the regret of our lifestyles and the choices we've made hold us in positions of paralysis, which keeps us stuck in our current conditions. Toward the end of my wilderness period, there would come another moment. It would truly be the last moment that decided my fate, whether I would die in the wilderness of my sins or thrive in my purpose. The thing about a wilderness is I had to want to come out, I had to want to be free, I had to want to be found.

Race

Whenever I have free time away from the busyness of life and can find a few hours of down time, one of my all-time guilty pleasures when I need to relax and cerebrally get away is to throw myself in the midst of a good movie, Not just any movie but a good one, especially a good crime saga, drama, or thriller, any movie where I'm forced to sit there and expend the corners of my mind. Trying to solve the main plot points of the movie is my jam. The very best movies are the ones that I can't even figure out, the ones that take me all the way to the last few scenes before I'm clued into who the culprit is. Those are my absolute favorite.

Other flicks I enjoy watching are those that involve a bunch of actors pitted against each other in a desperate dash to get to the hidden treasure. The film that quickly comes to mind is the movie *Rat Race* that was released in 2001. In it, the owner and mogul of a Las Vegas casino puts on this elaborate high-stake gambling game for the high rollers in the casino. The concept is to take six random and ordinary strangers and have them race against each other to retrieve two million dollars that is stuffed and hidden in a locker at a train station miles away. The only rule is that there are no rules. First one there gets the money. The movie, however, is twofold. While the competitors are racing to get the money, the high-rolling gamblers are also watching the whole race take place from a luxury suite at the casino and betting on which of the six competitors will get there first. It's a hoot to watch.

As I was thinking about this movie though, I started envisioning and internalizing it from the perspective of my own life. My rat race became my career, the gym, and nightclubs where I tried to define my values, build my self-esteem, and find my self-worth. In doing so, I became angry and turned to alcohol, drugs, and violence that led to my shame and becoming lost in a wilderness of regret. I had lived as Antonious long enough but didn't know how to find myself back to Will. My wilderness became all I could see. The embarrassment of my past and the deficiencies of my character clouded my ability to see a way forward. I didn't know how to see myself once I lost myself. What happens when we get offtrack of our coordinates? What happens when we lose ourselves in the rat race of life? What do we do when we're lost in the wilderness of life? How do we find our way home? I had to decide and answer those questions for myself, whether I was going to die in the wilderness of my poor choices or live in the next dimension of my purpose. I had to realize that my wilderness was a pit stop, not my final destination. Sometimes we need to see that our wilderness isn't meant to kill our souls, more so to activate our calling in life. I write this book with that purpose: to help others who may be lost or to help those to avoid becoming lost.

The Broken Piece: Regret

> Many of us crucify ourselves between two thieves—
> regret for the past and fear of the future.
>
> —Fulton Oursler

I believe the prophecy and potential legacy of our life can do two things through the wilderness: die or activate. Notice I said the word *through*. That's correct, my wilderness was temporary. It wasn't permanent. Being lost will look different for each person. My regret became just another prison. Antonious was my prison.

The reason I spent so long in my wilderness was because I regretted everything that had manifested in my life. Anytime I looked at the results of my life, I only saw my mistakes. I only saw what I unfortunately became. This can happen to a lot of us. We become too attached to our regrets that we often can't see our opportunities or possibilities anymore. We only see what we've done. Regret, by definition, is "a feeling of sadness, repentance, or disappointment over something that has happened or been done." This often is the wilderness where many people have lived or are living today—the wilderness of regret. It's often what keeps us from coming out of the season of being lost or coming in touch with our future. For me it was very much the case. I can't begin to explain how many of my birthday celebrations I never enjoyed because it would always put me in a position of reflection. And anytime I looked at my past or my life, I hated it. I regretted everything about it. I struggled to get out of this state for a long time—ten-plus years to be exact. Through the seasons of my trauma, my need for validation, and my time being lost, not only was I continuing to find more broken pieces, but I was also breaking hearts and relationships along the way. My brokenness soon became others' privations.

PART 4

&

Relationships

"The way in which two or more concepts, objects, or
people are connected, or the state of being connected.
The relationship between two people or groups is the way
in which they feel and behave toward each other."

CHAPTER 10

Church

One could say, with little exaggeration, that the
persona is that which in reality one is not, but
which oneself as well as others, think one is.

—Carl Jung

"I'm Christian," I would say if someone asked. But up until the age of
twenty-eight, my life did everything but resemble that walk. It's true,
I was a Christian and believed in God mostly my entire life, but my
relationship with God was the same as it was with myself: nonexistent. After struggling with thoughts of suicide and almost wanting to
give up on life, I knew I needed a change, but I didn't know what. I
knew I needed God but didn't know if he'd still recognize me. I had
been lost for ten years and needed to find my way back home.

Routine

I started going to church when I was four years old. At that
time, it was just my parents and my brother and I. My sister would
come a few years later and so would our dedication service. My sib-

lings and I were all dedicated at the same time on June 20, 1993. For those that aren't aware, a dedication service is a Christian ceremony in which the parents consecrate the children to God, as well as dedicate themselves in raising their children in the religiosity of Christianity. I was eight years old when my parents made that commitment over my life, and I'm forever grateful that my parents did. But back then, I had no clue what any of that even meant.

Growing up as a Christian in an old-fashioned church was something I never regretted. Like most kids, I typically saw church as an assignment, as a chore. In my household, it was a mandate living under my parents' roof. It was only later in years, and with maturity of course, that I'd come full circle to understand that the reality of church wasn't just about sitting in pews, singing a few hymns, throwing some money in a tray, listening to a sermon that barely made sense, or bowing a head for prayer. But it was about having an encounter with God and a relationship with Christ, which I'll get into later.

As a teenager, I saw church and God as structure and discipline, not relational or something transcendent. Church for me was part of a routine. I'm not just talking about Sundays either. I mean all through the week—Bible study, teaching classes, youth nights, prayer meetings, worship nights, and choir rehearsals, anything church related. And our family was there. My parents placed a high importance on my siblings and I being raised up in the church. In fact one of my mom's favorite verses is Proverbs 22:6, which says, "Train up a child in the way he should go. And when he is old, he will not depart." And like anything requiring training, it's through consistency, devotion, repetition, discipline, and modeling that are needed to fully develop the skills to grow and be good at anything.

While my parents weren't perfect—no family is—my parents ensured our home was a place where we served the Lord. It was even carved into the huge wooden plaque on the wall of our home.

But as for me and my household, we will serve the Lord.

—Joshua 24:15

But is that enough? Is it enough to wear the persona of Christianity without the relationship? Is quoting scriptures and posting it on social media enough? What about playing church and putting on the Christian persona? Easier than living it, huh? Even though I was raised in the church—even had it modeled for me at home most of the time—and though I attended all the traditional church gatherings throughout the week, church for me was more of an image than it was an identity. There's a big difference. Sometimes it's easier to appear one way and live another. I made the image of faith more conducive to my individual lifestyle rather than submitting my life to the creed of Christianity.

I fear some Christians today put on the representation of Christianity—talk it, walk it, and wear it. But when it comes to living it out, the authenticity of their spirituality seems void of Christ. I'm not judging, I'm exposing. I say this because it was very much the case for me. I played with it, but I didn't live in it. It turned out to be a routine of life more so than a relationship with Christ growing up. Even in my youth and adolescence, church seemed like another hangout spot and a safe place to go in order to keep out of trouble and high school drama. It was also a clear mandate of my parents' remember. So how was I to turn a routine into something relational and personal? I knew God as a child and in my adolescent years, but experiencing God is something entirely different. I needed an encounter.

Encounter

Church, back in my early youth, seemed different to me then than it does today. The encounters with Christ and the movement of the spirit through the church that I saw seemed more prevalent and profound then than it does today. Back then I saw church as something radical, on fire with crusade-like ministering. I saw alter calls that lasted for hours and hours. I witnessed people speaking in tongues and being moved by the Holy Ghost. I saw worship that would seem to go on forever with many people desperately needing an encounter with God. I saw people laying hands on each other during prayer and getting rocked by the Spirit. I saw people prophesying and declaring the word of God in the middle of sermons. I saw the move of God in the church without reverence of tradition, regulations, schedules, and preferences. I saw people crying out and confessing their sins before God without care of personal image or prestige. Back then I saw people rushing to have an encounter with God. Back then I saw the spirit of God show up in radical ways and transform the very hearts, souls, and minds of the congregation. Back then I experienced the spirit of God fall fresh on his people. Back then I saw a hunger and desire of people's hearts wanting a renewing of the Spirit and an authentic experience with Christ. Back then I saw Christ, not church.

I remember on one occasion during a sermon, the preacher stopped the sermon to address the sin that he felt was dwelling in the congregation. The pastor grabbed a trash can and lit the inside on fire. As the pastor began to speak with the anointing and authority given to him by God no doubt, the pastor began to challenge the congregation to confront their sin. The pastor challenged the people in that very moment to go out to their cars or dig into their pockets or even write it down on a piece of paper any sin they were being held captive to and bring it up to the stage and throw it in the fire. It was a palpable scene I could remember as people flooded the stage to surrender and submit themselves to God in that very moment. Back then I understood church. I understood the Christian movement. I understood that people wanted an encounter with God. I often fear and wonder of what I saw back then and what I see going on in the church today if we've gotten out of touch with Christ, if we misconstrued the perpetuity of the church from its early days, if we've stopped experiencing God and settled for experiencing a routine of church. Have we gotten comfortable with the routine of church that we no longer seek an encounter with God? Have we gone down the path of religion for too long and forgot what it means to have relationship with Christ? Have we forsaken the Spirit and the move of God for tradition, head count, prosperity, and image? Are we too focused on building the best power point sermons that we've gotten out of touch with evoking the Spirit, convicting the hearts, and exposing the sin of the church? What does it truly mean to say "I'm a Christian" today? During my high school years, to say I was a Christian was something I didn't do. Going to church or telling people that I was a Christian never seemed like the popular or cool thing to confess back then. While I saw a lot of amazing experiences happening in the church, to me it just seemed like a place to hang out.

Friday's

I think it would be fair for me to say that during my teenage years, I spent more time in church than any other place. Outside of going to family functions, playing football, or going to school, I was in church constantly during this time. I didn't mind it either. I honestly think it's where I started to compartmentalize the realities of my environments—meaning, I was one way at church, at home, and another way around my friends at school. Church, during these years, was healthy for me, given everything that was going on within my homelife around this time. With Eddie, Courtney, and my brother gone and dealing with my own internal conflicts as a growing boy, church seemed like my safe haven of sorts. At least that's what it turned into overtime for a few years.

I wasn't one of those kids that read the Bible. First off, I hated reading. I mean, I hated reading as a kid, so cracking open a book that I could hardly read, let alone understand, was something I just didn't do. I didn't enjoy praise or worship either. I just felt like I was doing something to follow along with everyone else. I didn't pray a whole lot as well that I can recall. Honestly, I didn't know what to pray about or who I should be praying to. But of course, nobody knew any of this because I did it all to fit in to the routine of my life. Remember, I didn't see church as relational. Therefore I never saw Christ in my personal life. But I would be at church nonetheless. My favorite night was called Friday Night Hangouts. I anticipated this night every month. It was the second Friday of each month. It was a night where my church would plan this huge hangout night for teenagers around the community to come out hang out, meet new people, hear a short ten-minute sermon, and spend the night having fun. There was everything there, basketball and volleyball tournaments, arcade rooms, café and lounge area, live DJ and dance floor, inflatables, and much more. It would only cost five dollars per person to enjoy the night of fun. I would have a blast. It never felt like church, just seemed like a really cool place to be on a Friday night. My parents never seemed to mind me going, plus it was a lot safer than the hundreds of other things I could have been doing at that time.

Growing up in the church comes with certain perks as well. The main one is that I knew everyone from pastors, deacons, elders, leaders, and their kids and was pretty close with them as well. This also allowed me to be a part of a lot of behind-the-scenes stuff with the church to help out with events like these and others. With events like Friday Night Hangouts, I would help with setup and teardown, give out name badges, greet people as they came, serve food in the cafe, manage tournaments, and a lot of other items. This also meant that I handled cash quite often. It was where I would first begin to rob the church. Around this time, I became extremely rebellious. This was in my teenage years where I was still trying to quantify what my identity was while dealing with the trauma in my life at home. It was my way of trying to garner attention. I don't know why I started stealing from the church to be honest. I never had a reason to. It wasn't like I was poor or anything. It was an inclination, and I just went with it. I always felt like no one paid attention to me, so rebelling became natural. I was becoming rebellious and angry toward much of life around this time. I didn't think nothing of it, I just did it. It's actually something that I've never confessed out loud, but it was always on my list of shame throughout the years. I didn't just rob the church during Friday Night Hangouts either.

During the month of June, my church would also own and manage firework stands to raise money for our youth ministry. I would spend a lot of days and nights there during these times to help out with the setup, teardown, food runs, selling, and manning the stands. It was fun staying the night in RVs, pulling pranks on our other locations, competing to see which stand would make the most money, and hanging out with other church kids. But like Friday Night Hangouts, it was a place I would steal cash secretly when no one was looking, not a lot but enough that would go unnoticed. It was all part of my persona. After all, who would ever suspect me of doing any of that. I fit in. I was a church kid. Don't get me wrong, I didn't go to church just to steal from it. It's something that became of my hidden persona, no excuse for it. It was the incubation of my becoming Antonious before I was given the name. It was the start of my persona.

Camp

Being a Christian as a teenager wasn't always just about hanging out, having fun, and stealing from time to time. There would also be moments of awakening I would experience as well. This would happen almost all the time during youth summer camps. It was two weeks during the summer where the youth ministry would load up about three hundred or so teenagers for a chance to meet new people, enjoy the camp lifestyle, get away from the parents and distractions of life, and hopefully have an encounter with God. It was a lot of fun. It was the only real time I spent away from my family for long periods of time during the summer months. Anytime I reminisce about summer camps with my parents, they always tend to remind me of how I would call them every Monday night while at camp to remind them to tape *Monday Night Raw*. I was a huge wrestling fan. Camping miles away from home without access to a television wasn't going to change that either.

Summer camps were like no other church experience I can recall. It truly took me to a place of absolute vulnerability and openness with God that I would not typically experience back home during my regular church routine. Summer camps were often the place where I would see the presence of God show up the most. Teenagers were on fire to know God in a deep, new, and profound way as was I. Being at camp took me away from all the distractions with home and family, school and friends, trauma and problems and allowed me to leave it all at the altar. There were many altar calls I'd attend because I truly wanted to know God. I had always known of God, but to experience God and have a relationship with him was something totally different. And at summer camps, it's what I wanted. Summer camps were good for lighting my fire and enthusiasm of having a relationship with Christ. But how do you keep the fire going when camp is over? That seemed to always be my problem. While I would go on too many summer camps and have an amazing time, my relationship with God felt like it never penetrated my heart enough to make it stick. I mean, I knew the stories. I knew what Christ did for me on the cross. I knew I should be praying and reading my Bible. I knew I should be memorizing scriptures. I knew I needed to be real about my walk. I knew my parents wanted me to go to church and have a relationship with God. But like I said earlier, I only saw church. I never saw Christ. I didn't know what it meant to be a Christian. But I guess I was one because I fit the persona. I never saw Christ because I never saw myself. And because I didn't see myself, I didn't recognize why Christ died on the cross for me.

Commission

I often wonder what Christ thinks of the church today. I wonder if Christ would be shocked or pleased with how much the church has transformed from the early days of his ministry. I wonder if Christ would approve of his movement that has radically changed the way it ministers his message. I often wonder if Christ feels glorified or mortified with how the church lives out his mission. I wonder this because we must remember, Christ never saw any church, Christ saw a mission.

Therefore go and make disciples of all nations, baptizing them
in the name of the Father and of the Son and of the Holy Spirit

and teaching them to obey everything I have commanded you. And surely, I am with you always to the very end of the age.

—Matthew 28:19-20

It's interesting for me to think that in over two thousand years, the church went from starting in small intimate homes to mega-sized buildings. The interesting part for me though isn't in where it started, it's in where it seemed to have stopped. Church today is all over the globe in buildings of all sizes, but sadly I fear and wonder if church and the true message of Christ ever makes it back into the small intimate places of our own homes or alone times. This is the point that I never recognized as a teenager or young adult. Church was never about a building; it was about people. It wasn't about an image; it was about humility. Church was never about comfort and coffee; it was about conviction and confessing of sin. It wasn't about numbers and attendees; it was an encounter and experience with God. Church was never about personality and social media; it was about being Christ ambassadors to the world. It wasn't about fitting into a persona; it was about being set apart for a calling. The church was about people and purpose to tell the message of hope, love, mercy, power, and restoration that comes with knowing Christ. As I got older, I'd often find myself attending church service, pondering these thoughts as I looked out at the crowd. I often wondered if I was just there to have an experience with Christ or an experience with church, never actually seeing the commission in between. I lived in the image of church more so than the image of Christ.

Religion

Ever heard the saying "Christianity is not religion because it does not involve humanity's attempt to reach God but rather God's attempt to reach humanity"? There are two distinct phrases I want to pull out of that text, which is "humanity's attempt" versus "God's attempt." Religion versus relationship—this was my dichotomy.

I spent years never truly having a relationship with God because I always saw my own life with shame and regret. And because I wasn't the perfect Christian who read the Bible, did my daily prayer, and lived without sin, I didn't see how it was possible to have a relationship with Christ. I was trying to reach God by works instead of faith, not seeing that God had already reached me through Christ.

Since the days of Adam and Eve, man has constantly demonstrated an intense effort to consciously deduce our own understanding of God's intent and Christ's works, thereby bending the word of God and the examples of Christ to satisfy our own lifestyles. I had spent years trying to fit God into my world and my box of understanding. It didn't work for the Israelites, and it didn't work for me. I believe religion is born in the gap between God's revelation and the suppression of revelation to Christians. So instead of filling the gap between the space with faith, obedience, and discipline, I filled it with false idols, sexual immorality, pride, and often my own religion, often making assumptions around God's purpose for my life. This I believe was the cornerstone of my religion. Jason and Ron Carlson put it this way: "A relationship with God will never be found in any religion because religion only offers swimming lessons to people drowning in the sea of sin." They go on to say, "The only hope for men and women drowning in the sea of sin is Jesus Christ." This is where we find relationship.

The issue that often happens, I fear, in Christians today is that we are too busy with religion, the traditions, regulations, standards, preferences, perspectives, and our own fluttering ideology of Christology. Therefore, often missing out in a free relationship and an encounter with God. This is what I meant when I said I only saw church, never Christ. Because church was forced on me as a kid, I saw it as such—something regulatory, never something to be made personal. It's not enough to know the Bible word for word, even the devil knows the Bible. It's not enough to go to church on Sunday, the devil is in attendance as well. It's not enough to call ourselves a Christian, even the devil was in the garden with Eve. The devil is just as much in our face every day as well. When we say we're a Christian, what does it mean? I had been living in religion all my life, calling myself a Christian, not ever realizing the significance of having a relationship with God. I thought if I read my Bible, pray, pay my tithes, and do godly type of acts that I was a Christian. I never took on the idea or attitude of having an intimate, everyday, one-on-one walk with God. Religion became my persona.

Museum

I often wondered if people knew how I lived when no one else was around. I often wonder this about people throughout congregations around the world as well. Who are we outside those church walls? Sometimes when I walk in a church today, either a mega-sized one or a smaller-sized one, I often get the sense that everyone has it together. I see warm hugs and handshakes, joyful conversations and smiles, laughter and warm receptions, and mostly positive interaction throughout the church. I wouldn't think this was a house of sinners but more so a palace for saints. I've heard the term once said that "church isn't a museum for saints but a hospital for sinners."—true, yes.

In theory, I believe this is what the church strives to portray. But in retrospect, I've been to both a museum and hospital and wonder if the church today is far removed from this dogma of being a hospital for sinners. Anytime I go to a hospital, I know what to expect—nurses and doctors running from room to room in a frantic haste; sick and near-dying individuals spread throughout the corridors of emergency rooms, hoping to be saved; patient's family members waiting to be informed of good or bad news; and staff working diligently to console or understand the needs of people all around them. The hospital is a place to stave off sickness and hopefully prevent death.

When I go to a museum, it's a completely different atmosphere—fine art and paintings covering the floors and walls; people slowly pacing the floors, marveling over the beautiful pieces of work; the monumental structure; order and cleanliness of the facility; positive interactions and celebrations over the experience; and staff members working with such pride, explaining all the intricate details of each masterpiece. The museum is a place to experience exhibited beauty of all kinds.

As I got older and entered my twenties, church didn't seem like a hospital for me, it seemed more like a museum in fact. Sometimes I think the persona of the church disarms the true nature of the church. Sometimes I questioned, if it truly is a hospital, why do I admit myself every Sunday? What care do I need provided? If it is a hospital for sinners, am I getting the proper dose of medication, or am I seeing the sickness of my sins dissipating? If it truly is the hospital for sinners, are we healing the sick, are we carrying for the ones dying of sin? If it's not a museum of saints, am I wearing my sin or covering it with a persona? Leonard Ravenhill suggested, "The early church was married to poverty, prisons, and persecutions. Today the church is married to prosperity, personality, and popularity." After my teenage years, I would leave the church and spend most of my twenties married to myself, my need for validation, and my season in the wilderness. I needed God but didn't know how to lose myself and this broken ideology of church that I had known for so many years. I didn't know how to find a relationship with Christ.

The Broken Piece: Persona

> One could say with little exaggeration that the persona is that which, in reality, one is not but which oneself as well as others think one is.

> —Carl Jung

By definition, persona "is the aspect of someone's character that is presented to or perceived by others." What I find interesting in this definition is the intentionality of the word and disillusionment of its results. I had a persona, especially when it came to being at church.

Like I said, I knew the Word, worshipped in front of others, prayed like everyone else when it was time to do so. But when I left, I blared my rap music, met up with my friends at the beach to go drink, and spent the night out partying. But I didn't miss a Sunday. For me, sometimes the persona of the church endorsed the persona of my character, I felt. In my eyes, the church never looked like a hospital the older I got. I didn't recognize that I was sick with sin or that others may be worse off than me. And because I saw the church as convenience, I had an attitude toward my sins that I could just address it later on, no need to go to the hospital. "It's not that bad," which is what I would tell myself. Even though I was sick with sin all my life, the culture of the church gave me a relaxed view of my brokenness. And instead of appearing sick because I didn't see a hospital, I appeared well because I was entering a museum. After all, who wants to appear sick and in need of desperate help? If I'm being honest, I think the biggest hypocrites are often found in churches today. And it's okay to say it. After all that's where hypocrites should be. But that doesn't mean we shouldn't call it what it is. It's okay, I was one of the biggest hypocrites out there. It wasn't until I got tired of living in the temporary comfort of fig leaves that I recognized I wanted real salvation and authentic transformation that I began to address my persona. I was tired of the pretentiousness of my persona but still needed to drop the religion and begin to experience relationship. Sadly it didn't happen at twenty-eight years of age. I did decide to rededicate my life to Christ and get baptized at twenty-eight years of age after living in the nightclubs, being behind bars, and living a life of sin. But that only lasted for yet a season. I soon would be back in the streets, still being Antonious, still up to my old tricks. Little did I know, God was there through it all. There was awakening on its way, but I wouldn't see it for another seven years. And sadly more relationships would be broken along the way as a result of my persona.

CHAPTER 11

Friends

No one enjoys feeling weak, whether it is emotionally,
spiritually, or physically. There is something within the
human spirit that wants to resist the thought of weakness.
Many times, this is nothing more than our human pride at
work. Just as weakness carries a great potential for strength,
pride carries an equally great potential for defeat.

—Charles Stanley

The palate of my friendships reflects the diversity of my exploits and
journey. I never really understood the value of true friendship until I
realized that I didn't have any. At the time, especially throughout my
twenties, friendship required something of me that I was never capable of giving—myself. It wasn't for lack of wanting friendships, it was
an inability to remove my pride from what was needed to have an
authentic and meaningful relationship. Don't take pity. Understand,
I use this to set a blaze of illumination to expose my ancestry view of
the word itself.

Definition

There is no denying, friends give the unequivocal power and meaning to a purpose-filled life. We all, as people, desire connection, relationship, relevancy, belonging, and aligning ourselves to individuals that compliment and elevate who we are, what we can be, and who we become. I believe friendship's true worth is in its ability to create a natural space that allows for an exchange of both vulnerability and acceptance. In that small glimmer of space is the freedom we experience every day to love and be loved by those we share our lives with, mostly free of judgment, persecution, condemnation, hate, and even jealousy. I'm talking about true friendship, not an "instant friend." These aren't built overnight or in a weekend. These are people we've journeyed with, cried, and laughed with, the ones that know our inner most thoughts before we speak them, the people we can call day or night, and they'll be there for us, the people we can always count on, and the ones we're willing to tell our darkest secrets to, the people that see our worth while accepting our flaws, and the ones that don't sugarcoat the message but tell it to us straight, the people that are willing to pick us up when we fall, and the ones that encourage us when the journey gets hard, the people that love us even when sometimes we let them down, and the ones that are consistently there to share life's most precious and distressing moments. The tender cost of this affable transaction is not that of gold, silver, or copper but that which in its purest form comes in monetary heartstrings. So be wise to choose friends wisely because not everyone is meant to fill those shoes. Not everyone is called to be our friend.

Friend, by definition, is "a person whom one knows and with whom one has a bond of mutual affection, typically exclusive of sexual or family relations." When I read this, and I have to be honest, I've always used the word like everyone else did but never knew the depth of the letters as it's written. As I read the definition, a few words leaped out at me: "bond of mutual affection." So I dug deeper to understand what these words mean. Bond is that which "ties or fastens things together," and mutual affection states "a relation of affinity or harmony between people; whatever affects one correspondingly affects the other," This means our pains, failures, joys, burdens, tears, fears, anxieties, passions, losses, and wins are shared in concert with that of a friend. These experiences are the very things that bind us together, it's what defines us as friends. Without that level of depth, experience, consistency, and perseverance, we can't merely call just anyone a friend. How many of us can say we share this bond of mutual affection within our friendships today? Do we consider this when we are calling someone a friend? Sometimes I think we give out this moniker too loosely. Sometimes I believe our desire for friendship outweighs our purview of its meaning. It did for me for years. Often the friends that I longed for got replaced by the ones I settled for.

All through my twenties, I missed the ideals of what true friendship meant. I had people that admired my garden but didn't see or accept my broken fences, my broken pieces. Therefore I often unknowingly hid who I really was to get the friends or the appearance of friends that I really didn't need in my life. Sometimes my yearning for relationship exceeded often the value of the friendship. I'm not here to question our friendships, merely their significance, and ensuring we really understand who we are sharing our lives with. We can no longer afford to accept the appearance of false friends over the substance of having a real friend. Friendships are a necessity, not an accessory. I've known a lot of people over the course of my life, but my friendships were few until they were no more.

Chris

I've always been one to know a lot of people. But when it came to friendships, it wasn't my specialty. Over the years, I had people in my life come and go from early on in my childhood to later as an adult. I never had a problem making friends, quite the opposite. I struggled to keep friends for many reasons. First off, I had trauma from my early years that never got addressed. This caused me to be distant and gave me the ability to disengage from friendships easily, not recognizing their value at times. Second, as I grew up, I struggled to find myself, and therefore the people I knew were based on the environments and the stages of life rather than my values and standards in life. Thirdly, I chased success and valued money and the comfort that came with it over family and friends. I never invested the time into the friends I could have had. Now don't get it wrong, I very much desired friendships and the deep-seeded intimacy that came with them. But over the course of my life, I struggled with the vulnerability that's often needed in having friendships that have purpose.

Throughout my life, I would come to have many people I knew of different backgrounds, races, ages, and other attributes. I would find them everywhere I went, whether it was in my childhood growing up, when I was playing football, in my career, working out in the gym, spending time in the church. I knew a lot of people. People liked me, but I fear some never truly knew me. Sometimes our friends can be connected by the age and stage of our life rather than our lives themselves. Some friends are only meant for certain seasons of our lives, and others may journey with us through them all. We must at times recognize the stage of life we're in and ask ourselves who are meant to ride with us. I believe this is what I struggled with, who I was, and who were my friends.

Chris was my childhood friend. We met when I was in middle school. We became friends over a fight he had gotten into, well almost gotten into. During middle school years, Chris wasn't very popular. In fact he got picked on a lot by bigger kids because of his size. Chris was fairly smaller than most kids our age during middle school years, so it happened frequently. I never picked on him, but I would always see others messing with him. It bothered me a lot, but I didn't know the kids nor Chris, so I didn't pay it any mind. I had another friend in middle school name Carl. He was like the class clown. Carl always had jokes and used those to make fun of other kids. It didn't bother me because Carl knew not to joke with me. On one day, Carl and I were walking home from school when we spotted Chris walking home alone, so Carl decided to start making fun of Chris as we walked behind him. I always found joking harmless in my eyes, because after all they were just jokes. But that day, Chris didn't see them as just jokes and became upset with Carl. Keep in mind though, Carl was twice Chris's size. As Chris continued to get upset, Carl continued to egg Chris on and tell even worse jokes about Chris's mom. Remember those yo mama jokes? Carl had a plethora of them I could recall. I always wondered where Carl would get his jokes from because he was never on empty.

As we continued to walk, the insults got worse, and it was clear to see Chris's blood starting to boil over. But Chris would just curse back at Carl and threaten him. But that was it, which didn't faze Carl at all. It only intensified the bullying. Carl started to push Chris in the back to get Chris to fight him, but it was clear that Chris didn't want to fight Carl, given the size difference. To this day, I don't know why I cared. But it began bothering me watching Carl continue to push and egg Chris on. I took pity on Chris. He was defenseless and seemed ill-equipped to defend himself. I eventually told Carl to cut it out and leave the kid alone, but Carl's insults continued to berate Chris as he walked home. Chris finally got the courage to get into Carl's face, but Carl quickly pushed Chris to the ground. I knew Chris was no competition for Carl, so I got into Carl's face and told him to stop messing with Chris. Carl asked if I was going to have Chris's back, and I said yes. I pushed Carl and told him to fight me instead. Carl declined and started walking home by himself. I ended up walking home with Chris. I soon found out that Chris lived a block up the road from my house. After that day and overtime, we became friends. We had a lot of things in common as kids, such as watching wrestling, riding bikes, playing sports, video games, and more. Chris would either hangout over at my house, or sometimes I'd hang at his house.

The bullying never stopped for Chris. It even followed him to high school. But I was always there for him, and people would eventually realize that I'd have his back. We were as opposite as could be in terms of stature, popularity, and reputation, but we shared mutual interest, care, and respect for each other. So we never paid attention to our differences. It was those simple similarities that made up our friendship. Chris's parents got a divorce in high school, so Chris decided to stay with his mom who eventually moved away. Chris and

I tried to stay in touch over the years, but as I grew up and changed, so would my perception of our friendship. I was Antonious now, not the little kid who Chris grew up with. I don't think Chris understood that, nor was I ever in my right mind to ever explain it. I never saw any value in our friendship after high school. I was a different person after Chris left. Through the years and on most holidays, such as Thanksgiving or Christmas, Chris would always stop by my parents' house to say hi and see me to catch up. Eventually I wouldn't be at my parents' house anymore, and I'd stop taking his calls. My lifestyle had changed, and I didn't see that Chris and I had anything in common. I had moved on from that friendship. I lost being able to see the value of that friendship. The pride of Antonious and who I was becoming overshadowed it.

As I grew up and went on to face many different stages of my life, I often struggled to maintain those friends, never reaching the potency of having "mutual affection" in certain relationships. This was also indicative of me maintaining serious relationships with women, but let me not jump ahead.

Jason

I met Jason in church. He was a lot older than me and became like an older brother for me during a time when I was truly lost—the end of my teenage years heading into my young adult years. Jason was a rare friend, not because he was a church guy but because he seemed to get me. On many occasions, Jason saw me blow up on people or lose my cool, even at church, but was always there to have my back and understand me. Jason never judged me but always encouraged me to deepen my relationship with God and find my purpose. But during those years, that was the farthest thing on my mind. But Jason was consistent in helping me stay on track. He became close with my family and was always around if I needed him. Jason was good on cars as well, so anytime my parents or I had issues with the cars, Jason was always there to give a willing hand. Jason was the first demonstration of what true friendship was about, but I was in no place to value his friendship at the time. I was still in search of me, not really in search of investing in friends or people. Jason was the first person to introduce me to Christian rap music as well. I still listen to some of that music today. When I started living my life in the streets, my relationship with Jason began to deflate as well, primarily because I stopped investing. My path had gone in a different direction.

I had gotten to a stage where I had fallen into the John Wayne syndrome that I got to the point where I told myself I didn't really need others to be successful in life. But it was clear my barometer was off. See, I had overcome so much adversity in my life on my own. I saw friends only as moments in time, not companions of moments. We aren't meant to do life alone, but often that was my choice. But we aren't meant to do it with everyone either.

Tiki

Around the time I was twenty-three years of age, I was playing semipro football. Tiki played on the same team as me, and we began to hang out more and more after practice and football games. Tiki and I clicked because that was around the season I started drinking and going to bars more heavily. We were no good together, constantly getting into bar brawls with people and just being overall reckless. Tiki and I would always plan house parties or summer barbeques. But somehow those would end with some kind of violent altercations. Tiki and I just always had each other's backs. Whether it was him or me about to fight, we'd be there in an instant. But like many of my friendships over the years, it came to an end. Unfortunately and ironically, our friendship ended in the way it once blossomed, with me getting into a fight with him during a night out at the club. It was a misunderstanding that made me attack him, but our friendship was never the same after that incident.

As we age and mature, so do our morals and standards. Be wise as not to be foolish with who you call your friend. Sometimes we must distinguish when to leave friends in our past stages and when to make new friends in our future stages. We must not compromise our promise serving our friends' purpose. We may end up losing out in the process. I love that old saying: "Show me your friends, and I'll show you your future." My friends were a reflection of my lack of identity, often using those relationships to define my purpose during whatever stage of life I was in.

Men

Over the years, I struggled to find, attain, and keep great friends. I struggled with this for three main reasons, and I'm sure other men may be able to relate. First point I believe as to why I struggle with this is in my upbringing. The view of man-to-man relationship wasn't always something present in my household growing up. Most often, I was taught hard work—be tough, pick myself up, taking care of "self," and don't cry. Themes such as vulnerability, opening up, expressing myself, and intimacy weren't shown in my home. I didn't grow up around a lot of male bonding. I saw more pride than I saw humility or openness.

My dad was a military man and very stern. My dad was old-school and raised us up to say "yes, sir" and "no, ma'am." My dad was a man of much pride. My dad was a hard worker and taught us to be the same. He didn't like laziness and rarely ever settled for excuses. He showed us more about discipline, respect, and hard work than he did about love, emotions, and hugs. All the hugs in the world from my mom didn't fix this either.

I believe this is why it's more natural for women to display because we see it in mothers. And because it's often easily displayed in women, we label it as feminine to have such emotions. So instead of allowing the substance of these characteristics to take root in our lives, we shelve it for the sake of putting on more manliness. This idea of putting on manliness becomes the center of our identity. And therefore our ability to display intimacy is negated by our pursuit to show our masculinity. This is why I also struggled in my relationships with women, because while they were asking and craving for more intimacy, I kept on applying more masculinity instead. Speaking from experience, it's not easy to put on something I was never taught or shown.

Second point I want to make here is the simple fact that men don't talk to other men, we just hang out with them. As I got older, I realized the guy friends that I had I didn't really know because we didn't talk. When I say talk, I'm not talking about sports, weather, or the news, I'm talking about matters of the heart. Our time and conversations together as men were often based on the nature of the surrounding activities. Whether it be watching sporting events, going hunting, boating, camping, having a few drinks at the local tavern, we often didn't get too deep into the most intimate things that were on our hearts. Often the activities themselves became the basis of our relationship. My friendships therefore settled on the mutual affection of our natural proclivities rather than the openness of our hearts' sensitivities as men.

In the *Disciplines of a Godly Man* book by Kent Hughes, he states, "We all know that men, by nature, are not as relational as women. Men friendships typically center on activities, while women revolve around sharing. Men do not reveal their feelings or weaknesses as readily as women. They gear themselves for the marketplace and typically understand friendships as acquaintances made along the way rather than as relationships. Also, men fear being suspected of deviant behavior if they have an obviously close friendship with another man. And of course, there are some who suffer from the John Wayne delusion that "real men do not need other people." That last part of the quote takes me to my third and last point, this idea that we, as men, don't need others in our lives, that we are good all by ourselves. This is what I thought. After all I didn't see it displayed any other way.

I fear that men today will settle for isolation rather than opening up and having relationship. I did for a number of reasons: my trust issues, past hurts, past shame, too many insecurities, imposter syndrome, misguided understanding of real masculinity, or just my inability to confront my social awkwardness. I was too busy building high walls instead of narrow bridges for others to see and hear my hearts cry. My heart yearned daily for the very thing I starved it from because of what I told myself about who I was. The real deepening fact here, and I want us to get this deep in our core, is that we can't validate our masculinity without other men in our life. The measure of a man's masculinity is not in what one can create for itself but of what he can sacrifice of himself to those around him. The friendships I had in my early years benefited me and the season I was in. I wasn't willing to sacrifice my pride and selfish mindset to see the true value of having friendships.

Christina

I met people in every place one could think of throughout my life—from the streets to the church, in business to the jail cell, at the nightclub to the football field, on different continents or even just taking walks in the park. People were easy to meet, friends were not easy to keep. Christina was a person I met out at the nightclub called Copper Cart. She was a bartender when I met her. We actually didn't hit it off at first, given that we both had very strong personalities. At the time, Christina was dating the DJ of the nightclub she worked at, his name was Med. I knew Med well because he'd buy cocaine from me every so often. On this particular night out, Christina and Med got into a heated argument. I happened to be outside when she decided to grab a smoke. Christina began downloading everything to me, even shed a few tears while she was telling me the story of what was going on between her and Med. Copper Cart was a club I frequented often to party and sell drugs with the crew that I ran with, so I'd always see Christina. And overtime we became super close friends.

I never thought I would ever meet someone in that environment that I would call a friend, but Christina was truly that, a friend. In the short amount of time, we knew each other. We had experienced so much in life and supported each other through it all. When I went to jail, Christina was there. When Christina's dog was dying, I was there. When I got into fights, Christina was there. When Christina got in a car accident, I was there. When I contemplated suicide, Christina placed the call. When Christina was too drunk to drive, I was there.

When I got baptized at twenty-eight years of age, Christina was there. The list goes on. Christina was even close to my family, even managed to get both my mom and sister drunk on separate occasions, unintentionally of course. Christina and I had a lot in common and was someone I shared some of my darkest pains with because I knew she'd always be there for me and never judge. Christina was actually the first person I smoked weed with after managing to never try drugs my entire life. But because Christina and I had so much in common, we got into a lot of heated arguments over silly things. We were both hot heads, and it didn't take much either. Sadly our friendship would end over a confrontation that went too far.

It was on my birthday actually. At the time. I was dating a girl. And for some reason, these two didn't seem to gel, and it was clearly apparent this night. It was my birthday but wanted to do something small with a few friends and family members, nothing crazy like years prior. By the time I showed up to my birthday party, Christina was already loaded from the alcohol. And I knew when I got there that she was already on edge. I knew Christina for years, so I knew all her tells as she knew mine as well. As soon as I arrived with my girlfriend, Christina got up and went outside to smoke. It was clear to everyone that she was upset. My sister was at the party and told me not to worry and that she would go check on Christina and try to calm her down. My girlfriend said that she wanted to go talk to Christina and clear the air, but I told her that it wouldn't be a good idea. And boy, was I right about that. My girlfriend ignored my warning and confronted Christina on the sky roof where I was having a small intimate birthday celebration. The talk between them didn't last long, and I went out there to break it up before it exploded in public because I knew how Christina could be, and I knew that my girlfriend wouldn't have backed down from her.

We soon decided to move the party to the next phase of the night, which was at a nightclub. But we never made it. Christina wanted everyone to stop at her house for some drinks so that she could change before we headed to the club. Christina lived right down the street from the club anyways, so everyone was okay with it. But I didn't realize just how drunk Christina was. Her boyfriend at the time was doing his best to get her under control. But when Christina drinks, she can get on another level as do I. As we were drinking at Christina's house, waiting for her to change, she started going off on me, calling me every name possible and telling me that I wasn't a good friend and that I didn't have her back. Christina communicated that my girlfriend didn't have any right to be in my life because Christina didn't approve of her and that I had her back and not hers. My patience was slowly getting away from me, and my pride was setting in. But Christina continued to get louder and more vulgar by the second and eventually started getting in my face, cursing and screaming. Her boyfriend was trying to hold her back, but she kept coming at me and yelling. I eventually lost my tolerance and pushed Christina back. But I push her harder than expected, and she went flying backward. My sister and my girlfriend grabbed me quickly while others were trying to calm the situation down. I went to help Christina up as I knew I should have never laid hands on her, but Christina and her boyfriend were upset and threaten to call the cops on me. I soon left with my girlfriend and others. My sister stayed with Christina to make sure she was okay.

My intentions were never to hurt Christina but to simply get her out of my face. But it still wasn't okay to put my hands on her like that. After all I knew Christina was drunk, and I should have never taken anything she was saying personally. It would have blown over, and we could've talked it out the next day like we'd often do. That incident destroyed our friendship. I never thought that night would be the last time we would see each other after everything we had experienced together, but it was. I reached out to Christina the following day and asked her to forgive me but never heard a word back. I allowed my pride to get in the way of our friendship. I removed Christina from my life with just one push.

The Broken Piece: Pride

No one enjoys feeling weak, whether it is emotionally, spiritually, or physically. There is something within the human spirit that wants to resist the thought of weakness. Many times, this is nothing more than our human pride at work. Just as weakness carries a great potential for strength, pride carries an equally great potential for defeat.

—Charles Stanley

While I've touched on a lot of key words in this chapter like vulnerability, intimacy, openness, mutual affection, and others, often why, I believe, I struggled too deeply connect with my friends and people around me is because of my pride, my unwavering unwillingness to get out of my own ways as Antonious so that I can step into the lives of others and experience life together. I became so self-involved at times that I lost sight of others around me that I shared my life with and what truly mattered. It's pride that often keeps us too busy, too opinionated, too sensitive, too judgmental, too selfish, too overly critical, and more. Remember, I'm in the business of chopping at roots. Let's not spend too much time thinking about the branches. I struggled with attaining friendships—deep, meaningful friendships—because I often wanted my friendships to be on my terms. Fact: Like everything else in life, I wanted it my way. If I'm honest, the fights I got into with friends, family members, coworkers, or others were simply due to my inherit pride that I wouldn't lay down at the sake of losing a battle or argument or the possibility of someone hurting me. This is why I often couldn't keep friends, because to experience true friendship, it calls for mutual affection. Simply put, friendships don't have room for our pride. This was my problem: My pride got in the way of experiencing true friendship and also destroying the friends I had. I wanted friends, but I didn't know how to let go of who I've always been. That was my work. This broken piece of pride that dwelled within me needed to go in order for me to have a friend. But pride didn't just interfere with my friends, it decimated my relationships with women.

CHAPTER 12

Women

It's tougher to be vulnerable than to actually be tough.

—Rihanna

The only women I ever loved, I lost. It's true what they say, "You'll always lose that which you don't value." Unfortunately, I didn't hear those words until it was too late. But before I tell that love story, I must disclose the man I was, the man I allowed every woman to see but also the man women could never truly know. It all started from back where the heart went cold. My heartbreak from Courtney would be the catalyst for my imperviousness toward love and my calamity with women.

Mask

It's easy for me to say any women that ever loved me never really knew me. It wasn't for lack of trying either. It's simply because I only allowed women to see what they saw, what I displayed. I only allowed women to see what was appealing to the eyes. A strong black man with a successful career, financially stable, athletic body, articulate, along with eloquent manners with savant-like characteristics to woo any women off her feet. I made it look good. I made it look real. But deep down inside, I was already dead, so were the words I would tell women. But none could tell.

It wasn't what I wanted to do or be, I didn't plan on being broken. Overtime I just naturally found ways to hide myself, to hide my broken pieces. I had played this game far too long to ever change. Life had taught me two very important lessons when I was young that I never reconciled with: It was that everyone eventually leaves me, and those that are close to me would eventually hurt me. I didn't want to experience that anymore, so I closed myself off. I got to a point where I accepted the fact that I had to protect myself because no one else was going to do it for me. The more I went on this way, the deeper the scars of past trauma became. But no one could tell from looking at me.

On the outside, I always seemed put together. But on the inside, I was a scarred little boy desperately wanting to come out, desperately wanting to be seen but too afraid to be hurt or disappointed or, even worse, allowing people to find out who I truly was. Like I said before, I had been hiding for years. I didn't know how to show my heart. I had covered it all up. I showed women what I wanted them to see because I didn't love myself to think others would love me just as I was, not only that but that a woman would stay around long enough to do so. I didn't want to tell people that I dropped out of high school and never went to college. I didn't want to say that I came from a family that was often dysfunctional and that I was embarrassed of at times. I didn't know how to tell them I had abandonment issues and needed validation to know that I was okay. I didn't want them to see that I was insecure about my identity and lived in shame from being behind bars. I didn't want people to know that I struggled with pornography as a kid growing up. I didn't want people to know I wasn't man enough to have kids so I chose to have abortions instead. I didn't know how to tell people I had anger management issues and often hid it behind the bottom of empty alcohol bottles. I didn't want people to know I was selfish, a liar, a cheater, narcissistic, and a master manipulator. I didn't want people to know that I was scarred inside and didn't know how to find my way out. I didn't want people to see that I was just like them. I didn't want women to know I was broken. I didn't want people to see the inside of my mess because I was afraid of the possibility of being rejected by others. So I hid. I showed women and everyone else what the world wants to see, because to lay my mess before others was tantamount to suicide in my eyes. My hideout allowed me to create a false narrative for people to accept me. But women were really never accepting me because they never saw me. I wanted out of this hideout, but it wouldn't be for about ten years until I'd see the small door opened to my freedom. But even that came with a price.

Conquest

In time I came to see that my hideout was destroying the very thing I was looking for in my life: love. I was hurting the very ones that wanted to love me, but I didn't see it until it was too late. I never realized there was great strength to be found in the wreckage of what we call weakness. I thought being tough and not having emotions was a good thing, especially as a man. It's what we're taught most our lives. It's our genetic makeup. Our masculinity is often the thing that defines the nature of our manliness. Take it from me, it's very much the opposite.

I've been in and out of relationships most of my life, often stepping into another one before the one I was in had even expired. Yes, that means I was a cheater, not glorifying it but calling it as it was. I didn't see women as assets of love. I saw them as missions of conquest. It was what allowed me to always keep the door open to my escape. Women for me were momentary pit stops along the journey of my life. I never saw marriage, kids, or family in the picture. Nothing in my life taught me that. My life taught me that things aren't what they seem, and not everything lasts forever. So I never allowed myself to have hope or emotional soul strings to be attached to any woman. I didn't realize it back then, but it was truly a game. I saw women much as I saw life, something to overcome before it overcame me. I was never in it to stay around for the long haul. And even when I did, I spent time plotting a course to my next conquest before I could get hurt. Keep in mind, I didn't see it this way at the time. I just thought I wasn't happy in relationships or that I was never satisfied with the women I chose, so I would move on to the next one.

Looking back on it, the paint strokes of my relationships with women tell a different story, a broken reality of what my heart was doing on the backside of my actions. I was a runner, noncommittal, detached from my own heart in a way that I was unwilling and unable to give to others. Women were my escape. Women were in fact the conquest that covered my emptiness. Again, women didn't know it because I showed them everything they wanted to see in a man. It was why women stayed around because I gave them something to hope in. I was supportive, generous, kind, attentive, a provider, a protector, and more. But when it came to opening up or showing emotions, the well was dry. It wasn't that I was fake, I just wasn't all the way real. I was a good fifty-fifty split. I cared about the women I was with but only to a point where I couldn't get hurt. And when I felt I could or would, I would find a way out. It was why I kept my emotions close to the chest. It was why I would never experience true love until I realized it had already passed me by.

The conquest would in time become my consequence that would ultimately tie back to my brokenness. The reason I went from women to women, relationship to relationship, was because I was looking for love that I couldn't find in myself. Not only that, but I also sabotage love by telling myself it was ensuing pain. This is why I said earlier about being dead inside. I had killed off love before I could ever accept it, give it, or experience it. If I ever wanted to truly ever experience love with a woman, I needed to break down every wall I had ever put up. I had to change my view of myself and of women. I was going to have to really understand what it does mean to be a man for a woman. I needed to find the broken piece that was handicapping my ability to share in the proficiency of love. My conquest had to become finding my brokenness.

Shy

I remember the day like it was yesterday. I was standing at the airport sending her off as she stood in the line to go through TSA. The airport was abnormally busy that day. The line was about a mile long. I often wonder, looking back, if that was my chance to change my mind before she went through TSA to get checked in. I watched from footsteps away as she stood there looking at me with tears scrolling down her face. As I walked up to her as she continued to progress her way through line, I said to her, "You'll be okay. We'll be okay." I remember her telling me, "I can't do this, Will. I don't want to leave you. I don't know how I'm going to get through this without you." I continued to console her as she made her way closer to the TSA agents. I knew my words couldn't atone for the moment. After all it was because of me she was even in this position.

My heart felt cold that day, I could see my love for her, but I couldn't feel it. I knew I didn't want her to leave, but I couldn't say it. I knew I didn't want to lose her, but I couldn't grab hold of her. I remember standing there, second-guessing it, and wondering how our relationship got to this point. As she continued to stand in line, I told her I had to go. It was too hard for me to stand there and watch her cry in public over our love. I felt less of a man with every tear that dropped from her face. I turned my back on her and walked away. I had walked out on a lot of women over the years, but none felt as gut-wrenching as this day. As I continued to make my way out the airport, I could only picture her face full of tears, a face that was once full of joy and laughter. As I walked out the airport, there was an emotion I had never felt before and didn't quite know what it was. I felt like I had lost something, something very timeless. But I didn't know what exactly it was that I had lost.

"I see my whole life with you" were the words she uttered to me many times. I was her home. But now she was going back to the place she was raised, Hawaii. Her name was Shy, a picturesque, effervescent, doting, and nurturing spirit and personality with an infectious smile and luminous joy that would touch anyone instantaneously if ever in the same room with her.

I recall when I first met Shy, she was a waitress at the time. It was a sunny summer day. I was there at the restaurant she worked at, meeting up to have lunch with a friend that worked close by. Shy came to my table to take my order as I sat there, still waiting for my friend to show up. It was the smile that drew my attention. It was breathtaking. When Shy smiled at me, it was as if the entire fabric of the universe stopped at the behest of her grand expression. In my eyes for a single minute, Shy made me seem as if I was the most important person in her world at that moment. I wasn't a person that smiled a lot. My friends and family have always said this about me. But her smile that day made my face grin in a way that even surprised the contour of my facial structure. I was in awe of her from that moment. As she took my order and went away, I spent the rest of my time trying to figure out the power of her presence. Shy's presence may have departed from my table, but her aroma and essence stayed and danced around my senses. Her aura was that virulent, something I can honestly say I never experienced with other women before that day. The entire time while I was eating with my friend, I was trying to figure out how I wouldn't be able to leave without saying something to her or getting her number. I wanted to know more about her.

I never saw Shy as a conquest because I never had a woman make me feel the way she did from one small moment. I didn't know what to think of Shy. I just knew I wanted more of it, whatever pixie dust she was leaving in the air every time she stepped out of my presence. I had to get her number but had no clue how to do it, especially in the place of where she worked. So I made up this ridiculous story about losing my car keys somewhere in the restaurant and asked Shy if I could take her number down and call her later on in case she found them during her shift. It was about the dumbest pickup line I had ever thought of or used, but Shy surprisingly obliged. And needless to say, I was elated. My intentions had nothing to do with lost keys. I simply wanted to know her more. I thought about her that whole day. It was crazy.

There was a catch though. I was in a relationship that day when I met Shy, a relationship that was on the rocks at the time, but we had been together for two years so far. We had a place together, cars together, two dogs and an established lifestyle jointly. But I wasn't connected emotionally, so it was easy for me to leave that relationship. After all it's what I always did. Not a proud moment, but it was who I was at the time. I could leave a woman just as quickly as I met them. It was how I avoided ever becoming emotionally attached to any woman.

Shy, like most women, saw everything I wanted them to see in the beginning stages. She didn't even know I was in a relationship when we met. By the time Shy and I got together, I was already separating with my then girlfriend at the time. We were already sleeping in separate bedrooms, and I was getting packing equipment to make my next move to a new place. My girlfriend was devastated at the time. She didn't see it coming and even more so was complexed at how easy it was for me to just give it up. It wasn't her fault though. This was just what I did back then. And it wasn't the first time either. I never told women I was leaving them for someone else. I just left.

My relationship with Shy moved and grew quickly, faster than any relationship that I had previously. It all seemed so natural as well. Shy and I became inseparable quickly, moving in together only months after being in a relationship. We didn't waste any time. We couldn't get enough of each other's presence. Being with Shy, most times felt like we were living on our own planet. We could laugh for hours at almost anything. Shy was adventurous, always pushing me way beyond my comfort zone to try new things. I was pretty set in my ways before I met Shy, but she broke through those barriers quickly. What I didn't notice at the time, which Shy would eventually tell me later, was that she was trying to break down my hard exterior and open my heart. Shy was the only woman to ever call out my fake smile and my hardened demeanor. Before I knew it, Shy had me paragliding even though I was terrified of water and couldn't swim. She had me eating sushi even though I hated the texture. She had me smiling in pictures even though I hated to smile. And she had me in volunteering initiatives with children with special needs, which was something that I never thought I would do. I was hiking, camping on the beach, and any other weekend adventure or bucket list items

Shy had on her list. I had never experienced so much life in such a short amount of time as I did with her. Shy definitely had me open up in a way that I never thought I could be in years.

While the experience felt natural and real, I often would try to suffocate the emotions behind them. So I didn't allow myself to be too attached. But it was becoming harder the more time we spent together. Shy made me feel things that I always wanted but didn't know how to accept it. After all I was a guy on a conquest, always hiding who I truly was. I didn't know how to take what she was presenting. With any relationship, it had its challenges. Shy and I had our fair share. After all I was still a broken man, and she knew that but only to a very small limited degree. I didn't dare show Shy everything. After all I didn't want to lose her.

Looking back now, I wonder if Shy would have accepted all my flaws, all my broken pieces. But how was I to put out the raw me, the broken me, when I was so used to showing people what I only wanted them to see? I was scared. I was losing her at the same time I was trying to hold onto her, all because I didn't know how to break free of the old me. I really wanted to. After all I believe Shy was the first woman ever that was worth it.

Shy and I argued a lot though, mostly at my distant nature and the ostensible fact that I was hiding who I truly was. Shy would say often, "You don't value me," or "why am I not enough for you?" "Why are you hiding stuff from me?" The truth was I was emotionally unavailable. Shy wasn't the problem, it was me. I always portrayed this strong image of masculinity, never allowing her to see my heart. Shy was right, there was nothing she could do for me to give her the love she deserved or wanted. After all I didn't love myself enough to give me a fair chance. What luck did she have with me?

I truly did love Shy, but I didn't fight hard to make it work. If anything, I sabotaged our love. I put Shy through a lot. Shy found a list of women on my phone I had sex with, pictures of my ex that I had saved. Shy took my verbal abuse and constant manipulation. I often made her feel like she wasn't enough when we were in public together. She found pornography on my phone. And when she got pregnant, I didn't support her choice to keep the kids. Eventually, Shy got abortions.

When I met Shy, she was full of life, found joy in the simplest of things, always smiled, and always tried to see the best in everything and everyone. By the time our relationship was coming to an end, Shy had contemplated suicide, lost her joy, always in tears, and had no purpose in life. Did we share joy, love, and laughter? Yea, we did, a lot of it. But my brokenness shattered her wholeness that I had once met. Did Shy have problems? Of course. No woman is without her flaws. But I know the intentionality of her heart for me was truly pure. I know Shy just wanted to love me even when I didn't love myself. But no woman ever knew the risk that they put themselves in by falling in love with a broken man.

The worst part of this diary entry was that Shy never left me. I don't know if Shy would have ever left me. I left her. I broke her, and then I left her. I ended the relationship with Shy, not for another women this time and not because I didn't love her, but because we became two broken people trying to hold together a broken relationship that was once built on a foundation of love and joy, now stood only sorrows and pain. I convinced myself and her that we were better off trying to fix ourselves outside of the relationship. The truth was I was still running. Only now I was running away from the mess I created. I didn't know how to fix what I had now broken. Not only was I broken, so was Shy, and so was everything we spent those years building together. I lost the only woman I ever loved. When I said bye to her at the airport as she was moving back home to Kauai, I remember saying to myself, "Don't let her go. Tell her how much you love her and that you couldn't see your life without her. Tell her you're sorry, and tell her your truth. Tell her how you truly feel. Be vulnerable and open up one time and allow her to see your true heart." I didn't say those words. In fact I never said anything. Shy got on the plane, and I went home.

The Broken Piece: Vulnerable

> It's tougher to be vulnerable than to actually be tough.

> —Rihanna

By definition, vulnerable is being in a position "susceptible to physical or emotional attack or harm." Another reads, "someone who is weak and without protection, open to attack or damage." If I were to list all the words that I could to define me, this wouldn't be one of them, this idea of vulnerability left in my teenage years. And I didn't have a clue how to get it back. See, vulnerability is enigmatic of itself. Vulnerability tells me that I must come as I am without covering and show myself to those that have the potential and power to hurt me—hurt me, inexplicably, if someone wanted to. This was my fear. I wasn't taught how to be vulnerable, and I sure didn't see it around me growing up. It only made sense, and it became easier to always reach for covering, to have a veil of protection over my heart. I had been hurt plenty in my early years, I didn't want that for my life. But here is the paradox of it all: Without vulnerability, I could never truly be seen. I can never truly experience love. I can never love and accept who I am. Without vulnerability, I can never step into who I was supposed to be or my purpose. I wasn't being tough by being invulnerable, I was forfeiting my right to live. All those years, I was hiding from the very thing I truly wanted: love. The brokenness, the conquest, the hideout, these were causing me to lose everything I wanted since I was a kid and never got. I just wanted to be seen, loved, and cared for. And all those that showed up to do it only became reminders of my past.

Throughout the span of my thirty-plus years, I had experienced trauma through death, abandonment, almost drowning, losing loved ones, heartbreak, and several broken pieces. My trauma fed my need for worldly validation, so I ran to a career with no values, to the gym in order to hide my low self-esteem, and into the nightclubs to prove I was worthy. But my running away only led to becoming lost. It led to my sinful and criminal nature. I found a new home behind bars several times and found myself on the brink of suicide in an open wilderness. Through those seasons, I destroyed and turned my back on friendships, walked away from God, and lost the only person I ever truly loved. All in all, I found myself in the valley where my bones remained dry. I needed fresh breath. I needed fresh life. I needed an awakening. I needed hope.

PART 5

Hope

"A feeling of expectation and desire for a certain thing to happen, a feeling of trust, optimistic state of mind that is based on an expectation of positive outcomes with respect to events and circumstances in one's life."

CHAPTER 13

Crash

I learned that courage was not the absence of fear but
the triumph over it. The brave man is not he who does
not feel afraid but he who conquers that fear.

—Nelson Mandela

Death came knocking on my door. It partially opened. It peaked
inside. It saw me sleeping. This death wasn't like anything I'd ever
seen before. I had talked to death many times through the course of
my life, even entertained it. But it never wanted anything to do with
me. This time was different. When death showed up, it spoke to me.
It said, "William, I'm getting closer. Are you ready to come with
me?" God had other plans though.

Forewarning

It was 2:00 a.m. on a Monday morning in June during the
spring season. While most people at this hour were nestled away quietly in their beds; head or face deep in a soft pillow; sleeping the
night away, preparing for another busy week. I was still up. This

wasn't a spur of the moment type of night, not at all. Actually it was a part of my lifestyle. Sunday nights were the last hooray to another thrilling weekend of partying. So often, though, how my night began wasn't always how it ended. Sometimes a storm will arrive when we least expect it. It did this particular night; my life would be forever changed after this event. Before I share how that night ended, I need to go back one month prior.

It was a Saturday night in May, around 2:00 a.m. in the morning, didn't seem no different from any other night. As usual, I spent that night hanging at the clubs with friends, drinking and partying the night away. It was just another weekend of escape. It was like most nights of fun but quickly erupted into utter chaos with a flip of a switch.

Typically when clubs closed, which in my area was 2:00 a.m., I'd usually get out quickly to head to my next spot. By 2:00 a.m., the club pushes everyone out the door and locks up its doors. The club may shut its doors, but the party continues into the night out in the parking lots and sidewalks. This night was no different. People were still outside drinking, chatting, bumping their sound systems, couples getting into arguments, while other people were grabbing food from the nearby hotdog stands or wait around for an Uber to arrive. It was always a wild scene. That was why most nights I'd get out of there quickly.

On most nights, cops were present in anticipation of having to either stop a fight, remove the crowds, or catch potential drunk drivers. On this night though, there was not a cop in sight, which I found strange at the time because anytime I'd leave the club, I'd always look to see where the cops were at because I was typically drunk or had drugs on me. This night, there was no cops. Usually I would always see one or two cops waiting around in the parking lots especially in this area of town, given how much crime happened during this hour. I never hang out around the clubs after 2:00 a.m. I knew nothing good came out of hanging around that environment too late at night. For some reason on this night in May though, I was in no rush.

Instead of heading to my car and getting out of there, I stayed around to talk it up with some friends. No harm in that, I thought to myself. I stood outside in the club parking lot, talking with friends and reminiscing on the night, laughing and joking while others around us continued to party, but I paid it no attention. Within the minutes though, the atmosphere would go from laughter and peace to tears and sadness.

As I continued conversating with the guys, out of nowhere, a fight broke out between two people. My friends and I stood there watching, seemingly unphased by the ruckus as I had seen it all before. As the fight progressed, looking out from my peripherals, I began to see other people running at haste to join in. I thought they came to break it up, but they just jumped in the fight. My friends and I continued standing there, watching the fight enlarge with more people as onlookers and others yelled and screamed into the scuffle for the individuals to stop fighting. My friends and I looked at each other instantaneously as if we were reading each other's thoughts. We decided to jump in the fight and help break it up especially once we saw guys starting to hit females. As the fight was beginning to simmer down, and everyone was trying to calm both sides down to understand the situation, before I knew it, gun shots went off.

As my back was turned when the first shots went off, I couldn't tell who was shooting or who the individual was shooting at. I turned around slowly, confused, and trying to piece together what was all happening as everyone around me began to run and scatter in different directions while screaming and yelling. I just stood there. It was as if my body couldn't move and was frozen in time. I could see the terror on people's faces while they ran for cover. To this day, I always wonder why I never moved, why there was no reaction, why there was no emotion. I was just in a silent pause as I looked on at the pandemonium. It was as if God was giving me a wide-angle lens view into the lifestyle and road I was going down. The only thing that grasped my attention in that moment was the loud scream of a woman. It was like hearing a mother cry for her child. It was a scream from a shattered heart. It would be the scream over the dying soul that laid motionless in the street.

As I saw the woman screaming and friends all around her, my attention drew to her focus. Lying there in the street, a body laid. I couldn't comprehend what I was seeing. I couldn't piece it together. I kept trying to solve for the last five or ten minutes, asking myself how could this happen. I just stood there, staring at the body, wondering who he was, if he was even a part of the fight. I kept telling myself, "I'm sure that man didn't come out tonight expecting this would be the end of his life." I was angry, sad, horrified, and at a complete loss all at the same time. The next thing that would catch my attention were the police sirens. Cops quickly swarmed the vicinity, hopping out of their cars with haste, most of them with automatic rifles or Glocks, no doubt looking for the armed shooters or potential witnesses. I knew the owners and security of the club that I had been partying at all night, so they allowed me to move back into the club until things settled down. The club security began to ask me what happened and if I saw anything. I didn't know what to say. It all happened too fast. I didn't know what I saw or didn't see. I was still in complete shock.

From inside the club, I could see the body still lying there while emergency crews worked to revive and stabilize him. Unfortunately, he never would wake up. He took his last breath there in the street. I stood there imagining his family who were at home sleeping and having to wake up to the news of losing a loved one. I imagined all the people affected by this man's life. I imagined what he did during the day before coming out to party that night. I imagined those friends standing around his body in tears, having to deal with that trauma for the rest of their lives. I imagined myself being the one lying dead in the street. My heart went out to all of them as I stood there. Don't get me wrong, I've seen many things like this happen over the course of time when I would go out, party, and stay late. But this was different. Everything about it felt different. It felt like I was in the middle of a moment. I was in the middle of a warning.

I finally ended up leaving the club and heading home around 5:00 a.m. after everything calmed down. It was a quiet drive home that night. My phone was ringing over and over again. People were checking in on me, I was sure, but I wasn't in the mood to talk. I was without words all the way home. Once I made it there, I just fell on my couch. I never did go to sleep that night. Something like that changes a person. It no doubt had an effect on me. I didn't go out for weeks after that night. I couldn't picture myself continuing to play in that environment and see dead bodies in the street at the end of the night. "No, thank you," I said. This event seemed like the catalyst for change, or at least it should have been. It would be a month later until I went out again, and that would be my final warning. It would be my last dance. It would be my final chance. It was time to decide.

Final

Going out on a Sunday night was always different than a Friday or Saturday night. In the nightlife, Sunday nights are called industry nights. Its typically the nights when the bartenders, promoters, dancers, or club employees go out to party and drink. The settings of those environments are usually smaller, and everyone knows each other because they're all in the same line of work and often frequent each other's nightclubs for special occasions or sometimes even just to hang out. That was one of the reasons I enjoyed going out on a Sunday night more than any other night, because I often knew the crowd I was going to be around was much smaller and filled with less potential drama. I also knew the house DJs on Sundays, so I'd spend most of the time inside the DJ booth, clowning around with them, taking shots, and having a good time.

Sunday nights where super low key. This night in June happened to be my first night out since the shooting, and I hadn't drink since that night either. So I was in the mood to drink and let loose, given my perception of the environment on Sundays. I was still a little on edge since the shooting. But the more I had to drink that night, the more relaxed I became. I was a heavy drinker most of my life, often drinking more than ten shots every time I'd go out, and I'd never admit to anyone that I was drunk even when they asked me. What's worse was that most people could never tell if or when I was drunk. Some people say they're a happy, fun, angry, or mean drunk. I wasn't any of those things. I would try my best to act as normal as could be. And usually I would try to monitor my limits, given the fact that I would always drive my car to and from the club. But monitoring my limits never really worked for me. This Sunday night was no exception. If someone asked me how many times during those ten-plus years I was drinking and driving, I'd tell them all the time. I was careless, prideful, and ignorant. My years of drunk driving and hardly ever getting caught only necessitated my behavior more.

The night was getting late, and the club was getting ready to shut down. I knew I had enough to drink and needed to get home. As I was heading out to my car, I spotted a few girls outside the club getting ready to leave themselves as they waited on an Uber. They, of course, caught my attention as I caught theirs, and we began to talk. Shortly after the pleasantries, I offered them a ride home, and we were off. As I was driving, they asked me to turn up the music. As I did, they began to dance in the car while I was driving. I didn't think much of it as I drove through the downtown city streets at now 3:00 a.m. I reached about sixty miles per hour as I was flying through the green lights, music blaring, girls in the car dancing, and me of course carelessly going about my life as I so often did.

It was as quick as a blink. It was as loud as a crack of thunder. It was as hard-hitting as a three-hundred-pound linebacker smacking me in the chest at full speed. I had somehow, in the midst of a sharp turn, lost control of my car at fifty or so miles per hour and smacked head on into a huge cement pole. When I came to, I stumbled out of the car, trying to ascertain what all just transpired. I checked on the girls quickly as soon as I remembered they were with me and at the time were dancing and not wearing any seat belts. Neither was I at the time of the crash. The miracle in that moment was that no one was hurt or had a scratch on them. The car looked like a folded-up accordion that had been bashed in by a baseball bat. I couldn't believe we made it out alive. When the cops arrived and saw the wreckage and took the report, they were surprised anyone had survived the accident. Even the onlookers that saw the crash were surprised we were all okay. I was ashamed, scared, and disappointed in myself. It didn't take too long after the cops had arrived that they identified I was drunk driving. I was arrested quickly and taken to jail. I couldn't believe it—first that I was alive, second that I didn't kill anyone, third that I was drunk driving again, fourth that I should have been in bed and getting ready for work in a few hours, lastly that I was going back to jail. This was the moment that transformed my life. It was the wake-up call that I knew was going to be the final alarm. I knew God was tugging at my heart this one last chance, hoping I'd respond. I knew that I needed to find myself. I knew something in me was broken. I knew if I didn't, my days were going to be shortened. Fear can be both a powerful mentor and deceiver if we don't understand how to wield it in our lives.

Warnings

Sometimes I saw it coming, sometimes I didn't pay attention. I believe the deeper I got into my depravities, the harder it was for me to hear or see the call that was tugging at my soul. So often I threw them to the side or took them lightly because I treated my life in the very same manner. Unfortunately, I was often too busy serving my own self-interest and motivations that I was almost willing to throw away my earthly value and my very own life.

I had received many wake-up calls throughout my life, some more significant than others. And every time I knew it was God asking for my attention and to throw off the decadences that I was surrounding my life in. Like Ludacris raps in one of his songs, "Why does everything that is bad for me feel so good?" I used to often wonder this as well. I chose to make and serve my own gods. We all do this, we just don't call them gods, but we treat them as such—our careers and accomplishments, our image and reputation, our marriages and relationships, our bodies and ego, and so much more. I strived and put countless hours into these areas of my life to achieve a validation. I had been drinking from the well for many years, trying to achieve some semblance of prestige, value, accolade, or purpose. And even when I did to some degree, it wasn't enough. It only compelled a desire to produce at more excessive rate to attain my earthly treasures. The fear of almost losing my life gave me hope that I could find my life.

The Broken Piece: Fear

> I learned that courage was not the absence of fear but
> the triumph over it. The brave man is not he who does
> not feel afraid but he who conquers that fear.

> —Nelson Mandela

Fear, by definition is "an unpleasant emotion caused by the belief that someone or something is dangerous, likely to cause pain, or a threat." Another one reads, "A distressing emotion caused by impending danger, evil, pain, etc., whether the threat is real or imagined; the feeling or conditioned of being afraid."

As I said before, fear can do two things: be a great motivator or a deceiver. I had both of these dilemmas at work within me. Fear motivated me because of two reasons. The first was because I was coming to the realization that I needed to change the trajectory of my life before it was too late. My experiences continued to convey that I was heading down the wrong path, that I was never intended to be where I was at. At least that was the feeling in the moment of my car accident. Within a month, I was in two near death experiences that could have easily ended my life at this time. Fear became a great motivator. My time wasn't up yet.

Second reason fear became a great motivator was because of my fear for God. My parents implanted the word of God in my life during my adolescent years, and it never left me. I think it's why it says in Proverbs 22:6, "Train up a child in the way he should go: and when he is old, he will not depart from it." I thank my parents for that. So how was fearing God a motivator for me? My respect and admiration for God were a motivation for me to realize that all those doors that had been opening and shutting all my life were God simply trying to get my attention toward a bigger calling, that the broken pieces of my life that I so long relied on were the same pieces God was using to sculpt a great purpose within me. I realized that it was because of the grace of God that I still had life. But then there was the backside of fear: the deceiver. Fear was also a great deceiver in my life for two reasons. First I didn't see a way out. I was afraid of what I would be or who I would look like without the fig leaves. I was so accustomed to my broken pieces; I didn't know how to wear anything else. More importantly, I didn't think others would accept me. I had to come to a place to accept and understand that all that didn't matter anymore. I had to have the courage to see myself in new clothes even in the midst of wearing my old scrubs. I had to have faith to believe that I was more than the subtotal of my broken pieces. I had to trust God to make me whole when all I saw in me was brokenness. Fear was telling me that I couldn't be anything more than what I already was. It was a great deceiver for many years. The second reason fear was a deceiver in my life was because I didn't know how to get out of my sin. Paul talks about this in Romans 7:15–24:

> I do not understand what I do. For what I want to do, I do not do but what I hate I do. And if I do what I do not want to do, I agree that the law is good. As it is, it is no longer I myself who do it, but it is sin living in me. For I know that good itself does not dwell in me, that is, in my sinful nature. For I have the desire to do what is good, but I cannot carry it out. For I do not do the good I want to do but the evil I do not want to do—this I keep on doing. Now if I do what I do not want to do, it is no longer I who do it, but it is sin living in me that does it. So I find this law at work: Although I want to do good, evil is right there with me. For in my inner being, I delight in God's law; but I see another law at work in me, waging war against the law of my mind and making me a prisoner of the law of sin at work within me. What a wretched man I am! Who will rescue me from this body that is subject to death?

This was my struggle. I didn't know how to get out of my sinful ways. I didn't know how to break the habits of my tendencies and the intentionality of my indiscretions. My fear was simply not allowing me to see God's grace and mercy. I was only seeing my sin. Fear was a great motivator and deceiver in my life for many years, but it was finally time for a transformation. It was time to address my broken pieces once and for all. Change comes with its own challenges, but I was at the point of my life that I was willing to accept them.

CHAPTER 14

Transformation

Faith is taking the first step even when you
don't see the whole staircase.

—Martin Luther King

Thirty-plus years since that initial trauma, and there I found myself
sitting in jail following my car accident. I was raised in trauma, but
now my life was surrounded by bars. It was as if my life had done
a full circle to this place of isolation, the isolation that once kick-
started my journey in that hospital room as a child. The only thing I
knew while sitting in jail was that I had survived the last thirty-four
years. But now I sit, needing a new kind of hospital, one that examined and traced the biology of my character and the genealogy of my
brokenness. This was my story. It was what led me to this place. I'd
had enough. I was through with this life. I realized there in jail for
the first time that I was broken but not beyond repair. It was time for
a new journey, one of hope and transformation.

Realization

I couldn't take it anymore. I felt like it had been fifteen years since I last experienced any real joy, since I had experienced life. I felt dead on the inside. And on top of that, I couldn't shake the undeniable fact that this was going to be my last year to live. My heart was heavy. Something wasn't right in my soul. I had lost Shy, then I saw death, and next I almost died. It was time to make a change. The walls were closing in. I could feel death living next door to me. I saw it when I woke up every morning. And I felt it right before I went to bed. I was living on borrowed time, and it was planning on expiring sooner than it was scheduled. I was scared. I had looked back on my life and saw that I had nothing to live for, nothing to show for all that I had done. I only saw broken pieces that lay in plain sight. I only saw broken hearts and promises that lay at my disgraced feet. I searched for hope, but it was off at a distance. My legs were paralyzed from all that I had done. I couldn't reach the hope that was predestined to be mine. I knew I was meant for more than what I had become. But how does one do good when all I knew was evil? How does one take off the old clothes and put on a new outfit? How do I retrain something that is already broken?

I spent fifteen years conditioning my mind, behavior, morals, principles, and values in the corruptible ideology of what I thought I wanted, only to realize everything I had made and become was worthless. I made up my mind there in jail, I was done being a fraud, a fake, a cheater, a deceiver, a trickster, a cold-hearted and distant individual. The only problem was how does someone transform everything that once was, everything they once knew? I had to break this cycle. I had to tear down my inner infrastructure that wired my system to be what it was. What I needed, I couldn't get off the shelf, I couldn't buy it at Walmart or online at Amazon. I couldn't order it through Alexa or have it delivered with FedEx. I couldn't find it in my family, friends, or loved ones. It wasn't at the gym, my job, or even at the church. I couldn't find it, because what I needed was already laid within me. I needed a new heart. I needed a transformation. But it was not as easy as simply making the decision to change.

It was about breaking down every lie and barrier I had ever created. I would spend the next year doing open-heart surgery. This would be the year that decided my fate. This would be the year I transform into life or into death. The grave had already been dug, but I wasn't ready to go in it—not yet. I knew it wasn't going to be easy, but I knew the last thirty-four years had a purpose.

Habits

I once lived for money, success, validation, pride, women, and of course anything that would scratch my ego. How was I now going to turn all that off? I once heard it said that "habits are your brain's version of autopilot." And that was very true for me. I had created a systemic inner culture of wicked and calloused habits that I needed to break free from. It was easy to say I wanted to change and be a better man, but I knew that the only way this would ever be was if I committed my life to this transformation. I had to be willing to put the work in. I knew I was going to have to forsake everything I once knew and everything I once was. I felt like God was giving me this last chance to either walk into my purpose or be laid down in my coffin. I chose purpose. But sometimes in order to step into purpose, we have to walk away from our inner inertia.

This wasn't out of need or desperation, it was time. I was spent and tired of being a charlatan, I wanted to finally be seen. I wanted to truly experience love. I wanted to finally be set free. For me, habits were like being in captivity. In order to loosen and break free from the chains of this bondage, I had to first accept who I was. I couldn't expect to change that which I didn't recognize as broken. It was hard, but I had to search my soul and the history of my life and take responsibility for everything that I did. It brought me to my knees, both in tears but also in prayer. I was often wondering how God could love someone so wretched like me. I even asked God this question a few times in my quiet moments. His response was classic: silence. Sometimes I think God's silence isn't because he's ignoring us. Sometimes silence is an instrument he'll use to develop us to trust in him. Once I was able to look back at all I had done and created, I had to share it.

For the first time ever, I started speaking to others about not only what I had done but also who I had become. Like it tells us in James 5:16, "Therefore confess your sins to one another and pray for one another that you may be healed." And Galatians 6:2 reminds us to "bear one another's burden and so fulfill the law of Christ." I spoke with people I trusted and even a few professionals because I couldn't do this on my own. I had done the lone ranger bit for long enough, I wanted people to finally know who I was. I wanted others to see and share in my story. I wanted to be healed. But first I knew I had to be seen naked and willing to lay down my pride and ego. I started telling people I knew I could trust: family, friends, and even church leaders. Almost every conversation, I was brought to tears. It was as if I could see the weight and burden of everything I had been holding on to all those years begin to break free from me. I felt like the fig leaves were starting to fall off me. I also reached out to Shy and others I knew I had hurt in the past to apologize for all the pain and destruction I caused but more importantly to humble myself and ask for forgiveness, even acknowledging that I didn't deserve it. Additionally, I started counseling after I told myself years prior that I would never talk to a counselor. Man, was I wrong. It was one of the best things I ever decided to do. It allowed me to be vulnerable in a way that I had never experienced before. I learned so much about the who and why of my habitual nature. Once I started to expose it, I had to begin to curve it. It would make no difference if I let it all out only to fall back into my old ways. I had to change it up.

I disconnected from old friends and acquaintances, stopped going to the clubs and bars, put down the bottle and quit drinking, changed the music I listened to, and put a pause on the dating scene. I had to literally do away with all the distractions I had been using in the past that allowed me to hide within the persona I had become. It was by no means easy, but it was necessary. Breaking a lifetime of bad habits, malicious tendencies, and other maleficence doesn't happen overnight. But I can honestly say that I never wanted anything more in my life than this change I had committed myself to. So once I had accepted my brokenness, exposed my sin to others, and broken away from all my distractions, I had to establish and incorporate new habits into the way I lived.

First I had to renew my relationship with God and make him a part of my life every day, not just on an occasion. I had to get out of my religion and start dwelling and living in relationship with God. I started daily prayer, reading my Bible, studying Scripture, absorbing wisdom from other great teachers of the Word. I began tithing and truly submitted my life to his will. I had done it my way long enough; I was ready to come home. Second I reduced my time in the gym and started picking up books to begin reading more. I was never much of a reader growing up. Now I'm in love with it. Third I spend more time with family. I talk with them every day now as opposed to once or twice per month like I was doing before. It feels good. Sometimes I wonder why I had stayed away for so long. But luckily I'm glad to have the time I've gotten with them back. Lastly I started being more intentional about the places I go and the people I spend my time with. This allowed me to be both present and vulnerable in those moments I have with others. And there were plenty of other things I began to apply in my life to break out of my prisons. But something was still wrong. Yea, I had taken a lot of steps toward change, broken old habits, and began walking in a new direction. But something inside of me was still not right. I'd seen flashes of the old me from time to time. I even came away from moments, still seeing the stain of my past attitude precipitating off my tongue and in my thoughts. The surgery, while in progress, was still not complete. My chest had been carved open and exposed, but I still needed a new heart. My transformation was still underway.

Crushing

There is no easy path to purification. The cleansing off of what I once was doesn't get done merely through fire and faith but also fight. It can seem easy to take flight and go back to what we've always been when opposition comes our way, but it takes fight to get to where we're supposed to be. As soon as we decide to change and turn our life around, that's when some of the strongest crushings will begin. I've dealt with impediments, difficulties, failures, and disappointments all my life, but it was different because I always had something to run to in order to ease the burden of calamities. This time, all I had was myself and God to confront myself. Sometimes I think that one of the hardest battles we will face in our lives is confronting who we are at our core. It's the place God wants to truly take us to conform our hearts to his likeness instead of the world's image.

Bishop T. D. Jakes authored a book called the *Crushing*. At the time it came out, I didn't pay it any mind to be honest, because I was still living and stuck in my old mess. I happened to catch an interview he was having with Steven Furtick about the book where he was elaborating on the idea of crushings and how God uses the pressuring of those crushing and traumatizing experiences in our lives to exact his purpose in us through those moments we face. It was as if T. D. Jakes was simply telling me that my story wasn't an accident, that everything I had gone through and experienced was for a bigger purpose. T. D. Jakes does a phenomenal job of exposing and justifying why God allows us to go through hardships of many kinds and how the purpose of our pain becomes the manifestation of our destinies. The only catch is whether we fight through the crushing moments in our lives or if we run from them. Because no matter what, the crushings will come. Mine had, and they would continue even in the process of my transformation.

Understand, once I decided to close the door on the first thirteen chapters of my life that you've been reading, opening the next door wasn't going to be easy. After all everyone only knew me as the guy I pretended to be, not the guy people read about today. People only saw what was presented on stage, no one had the backstage pass to my life. So when I decided to turn the page on life, most didn't understand. I wasn't shocked. I knew it would happen. After all people were hearing things that they couldn't believe was me or that I did. Some people stayed around; others left. We'll always lose some people in the spirit of the transformation, so that didn't surprise me. In fact I expected it after all I had done. Even my own sister questioned and doubted my ability to change, using my past to often remind me of who I was and what I had done, as if she wanted me to stay and live in that old address.

It would be a few months later from when I decided to change my ways that my crushings would resume. And this time, I had nothing to run to. I was determined to fight. The devil knew I was leaving the vocation of his classroom, and he was coming for me. I lost my career that I was at after seven years. my grandma Baby passed away. I became at odds with one of my uncles, it got so bad that he threatens to kill me in front of the whole family. People where criticizing and persecuting me over who I used to be and who I was trying to become. And the crushings continued to pour in. I couldn't believe it, it almost seemed like the perfect storm.

Then I remembered something, that T.D. Jakes book I had placed on the shelf months ago. It was like light bulb moment, the timing of that book entering my life and opening my eyes to who I used to be and what I was going through couldn't be any more perfect. Shortly after finishing that book, COVID-19 hit us all. It was weird though; I was prepared for it. Not that I had inside information or anything like that, but simply because I knew for me it was all a part of the pruning process I was already in.

The book did three things for me: gave meaning to my past, peace to my present, and purpose toward my future. Not only did I begin to accept and live in who I was and what I've done, but I also realized that there were more chapters of my story to write. At the time though, I just thought that meant figuratively, not literarily. But even on the verge of a newfound hope, I still struggled with five things that I couldn't shake. First, how was God going to use me despite all I had done? Why would he use someone who's caused so much pain? Second, I often wondered in the midst of my crushings if God had forsaken me. It was hard to know if God still saw purpose in me. Third, I was afraid I would go back. A lot of me needed to be reformed, but I didn't know if it would stick. I worried about the possible triggers that would go off and lead me back to who I used to be. Fourth, I was all alone. I didn't have anything or anyone to turn to. God had me in isolation, a place I never experienced before.

I often wondered and worried how long would this last. I struggled to wrap my head around the fact that God was pruning me. Lastly, I didn't know who I was now and who I was going to become. I was in a new territory. I was in the passenger seat of a car that wasn't moving. But God had the keys. I didn't know where he was taking me, but I knew that's where I needed to be. As the saying goes, the struggle was real. But if I didn't fight through the noise of my past, of my temptations, of the enemy's coercions, and of those around me, then I'll never get to the place I was predestined to be.

Trusting

Ever been in or faced a difficult time in life and go to find comfort in a friend, family member, or someone, and they say, "Just have faith, everything will work itself out"? That sentence always bothered me for some reason—"just have faith." It's like them telling me, "Well I don't know what to tell you. Just go trust in someone you barely know." It's easy to trust God until I had to. I had known God and believed in him all my life. But I never allowed myself to be in a position to trust him, fully trust him, truly submitting my life to his will and authority for my life.

The reason I struggled to trust God was because I was used to being in a position of control and power. It was how I functioned. I always did what pleased me. But now I had come to a season of transformation, a season I knew I had to fully trust God. Even in the midst of going through my crushings, I had to trust in him.

I truly had to let go and let God. Transformation requires trust but not in itself, not by my own power but by God. I had to accept that trusting God isn't about just saying it or even trying to do it on my own. It's simply allowing God to know that I can't trust him without him providing the strength to do so. In this, we find our faith. In this, we trust in God. For me, I had to realize that faith was about extinguishing the thought that I was capable. When in reality, I was unable to do so without God's sovereignty.

Isolation

To date, people are always shocked to know I can't swim, given my athletic prowess. But few people know that I once almost drowned as kid, and since then, I've avoided the water. It is a goal of mine one day to learn how to swim to conquer that fear. Being isolated underneath that water and almost drowning as a child, unable to use any of my abilities but simply sitting in a sea of unknown and having nothing or no one to run toward, was how I felt during the season of my transformation. God was stripping me of everything I've ever known—the gym, the clubs, the alcohol, women, friends, my career, and plenty more. It was as if God just wanted me all to himself. It was hard. I'm not going to lie. There were many nights I had to sit in the shame of my own misery, confronting the man I used to be, even coming to tears on many occasions, upset at how I got to this point in life and scared because I didn't know how to cope with this feeling of isolation.

We live in a world today where we hardly, if ever, experience isolation. Our phones keep us constantly connected to something or someone, and we are always attaching ourselves to some environment, entity, entertainment, or experience. It's often most of the time what keeps us from ever confronting ourselves because of all the distractions we put in the way. I can speak from experience. I always had somewhere to be or go, rarely ever sitting still to reflect on the man I had become. I didn't want to. I knew the picture was too ugly. I knew my canvass as a disgrace. I just kept busy so I could just paint over it. But there I was, the place that God wanted me to be, exposed and vulnerable. Sometimes moments of isolation allow us to see our natural fixations. By doing this, we begin to unlock and discover the intentionality behind our heart. Not only that, we begin to truly see what we value.

As I begin to see all these things, I couldn't believe it. Here I was thinking I was all that and a bag of chips, only to see that I was a frightened little boy. Isolation calls our attention. It won't allow us to continue to circumnavigate our life. It challenges our heart to be at attention. Sometimes I worry because I believe God wants our attention so he can show us our intentions, expose our afflictions, and reroute our direction. But we're too busy avoiding our isolations. It's exactly where I needed to be even if I felt like I was drowning, I knew the real miracle was that God had me the whole time through it. He's got all of us.

Write

I've never been one to write. In fact I hated it in school growing up. Over the years, I've shared bits and pieces of my life's journey with friends. Many times people would say to me, "Wow, you should write a book about your life and what you've experienced." I would hear it often and laugh to myself, thinking, *If they really knew everything about me and what I've done, I don't think they'd be saying that.* Over the years though, the more I faced and endured the experiences that I was in, and the countless moments of reflection I had to myself at times made me ponder the thought of writing about my experiences.

As I sat in jail, looking back on the entirety of my life, the calling to write a book about my life had rung louder in my heart than ever before. It was a constant beckoning on my heart to write this book. Like Moses in the wilderness, I challenged God many of days and nights, questioning, "Why would I write a book? Who is going to care to read my story? My story is full of mistakes, traumas, regrets, and failures. I don't want that exposed. What would people think of me if they heard my truth? Brokenness isn't a hot topic. It's not something that is trending or pleasant to talk about, why should I? I don't want to write my story, I'm not worthy."

Remember what I said about fear being a great deceiver. I hit God with every question in the book that I could to avoid this idea of writing a book. Again I didn't know how to write, didn't know what stories to tell. I didn't know who the audience would be. I didn't know anything, absolutely nothing about what God was asking of me to do.

So I took a step and another and another and another. I challenged God with every step I took, often not even starting to write a chapter until I demanded God to give me the content. Funny though, God provided, whether it was through a conversation with a friend, something I'd seen in a movie, a picture, something I read in a book, something I heard in a sermon, or something placed on my heart. God was constantly revealing stories, themes, and even the title of my book. I remember the morning, I heard it. I was up early working one morning when I decided to listen to a podcast. It was T. D. Jakes. He was doing a message called Mommas, Mentors, and Moments. It was an old message, but I decided to check it out nonetheless. As I sat there listening to the podcast, there was a moment where T. D. Jakes began to talk about how "your history has clues to your destiny." It instantly grabbed my attention as if again he was talking to me. He continued to talk about how God uses the afflictions in our lives to shape us. Then I could hear him through the podcast say, "I feel the Holy Spirit. Maybe it's somebody on television or watching on their phone, but I feel the Holy Spirit explaining some stuff to you. God cut you right there and pushed you in right there and shoved you out right there so that you can fit in a certain role that he is about to reveal in your life." I could hear in the podcast the clapping and shouting from the audience as the intensity and passion of his voice elevated with every word. I could remember my heart pounding and jumping as if he was speaking directly to me. I'd never forget those words, it was as if he had summed up the last thirty-four years of my life in those few sentences. I almost dropped to my knees in tears. He said, "So stop crying about who left, who ran, who stayed, who hurt you. It's just God shaping you to fit like a piece in a jigsaw puzzle into a place in the picture that only you can fit in." Then he said this, "I'm trying to tell you that you're broken in all the right places." It was in that moment that I knew I was called to write this book, that everything I had experienced or endured, that each mistake and misstep wasn't for nothing, that it led me to this point—this book to your ears. I just had to actually do the writing. I had to have faith despite not knowing the outcome.

The Broken Piece: Faith

> Faith is taking the first step even when you
> don't see the whole staircase.

—Martin Luther King

If there was ever a quote that perfectly described me, it was that one. My heart was hard. It wasn't my intention to grow up this way, it's what happens with years of bad habits, choices, and chasing the wrong values. It wouldn't be enough for me to just stop doing the things I did, I needed a heart transplant. The biggest focus of my transformation was on the inside, everything on the outside would follow suit if I got my faith aligned with God's word and promises. It's where all the broken pieces would begin to come together. It's where I allow God to take the pieces of this broken clay pot and reshape, reform, recalibrate, and make new what he already formed before the day I was born.

Understand, nothing I did or could ever do would surprise God. He wasn't worried about my debt because that had already been paid. God was chasing after my heart so he could begin to put me in place that which he already made. God had set me apart and made me for a purpose. But it was up to me to take hold of that promise. Sometimes though God will delay our promise to prune us to purpose. Every day God was and still is challenging my attitudes, my perspectives, values, beliefs, traditions, intentions, thoughts, my time, my investments, and many other aspects of my heart that needed transforming. It's not an easy or quick process. It's every day submitting myself to his will, even in my weakest moments, even when I don't feel like it, even when it's easier to have a bad attitude, even when it's easier to go back to my old ways. The maturation of my transformation was dependent on my dedication to my adaptation of God's fermenting process for my heart—meaning, God wouldn't force it on me. I had to want that encounter with him. Once I did, I had to have faith that God would do the rest.

Out of all of my broken pieces—and I had a lot of them—this was the most important piece. Once we turn over our broken heart to God, he'll restore all the other pieces along with it. The purpose of our brokenness reveals God's providence, so don't fret or be ashamed about it. God smiles and awaits our arrival so that he might restore us to his glorious riches. Paul prayed this very thing for us in Ephesians.

> For this reason, I kneel before the Father, from whom every family in heaven and on earth derives its name. I pray that out of his glorious riches, he may strengthen you with power through his spirit in your inner being so that Christ may dwell in your hearts through faith. And I pray that you, being rooted and established in love, may have power, together with all the Lord's holy people, to grasp how wide and long and high and deep is the love of Christ, and to know this love that surpasses knowledge—that you may be filled to the measure of all the fullness of God. (Ephesians 3:14–19)

My brokenness was never about me; it was about allowing Christ to dwell in the midst of my pieces. And it's there that I begin the transformation to become more like Christ and less like the world. Only then can I have true salvation, true relationship, true heart, and true transformation. This was my heart surgery, opening up and allowing Christ to change the characteristics of my heart. So what did all this mean for the future? Turn the page.

CHAPTER 15

Today

God can take broken pieces and turn them into masterpieces.

—Unknown

This story didn't end in jail or with me in a coffin. By the grace of God, I was able to see today. I was able to hope as well for tomorrow. God passed by me and saw all my broken pieces and simply said one word, "Live."

Pain

There were many days I didn't think I would make it. There were days I contemplated suicide, days I didn't feel I had any purpose to live, days when it seemed like it would be easier to give up, days when I felt I couldn't press on any longer, days when all I could see was my shame and my mistakes, and days when I lost all hope inside. I made it, though, when others thought I would fall off and go back to my old ways, when others didn't believe I would change, when others could only see me for the man I used to be, not the man God purposed me to be. I made it.

I knew that my story had more purpose despite my past. I knew that my pain was the entryway to my promise. I knew that the pattern of my life was the training grounds toward my new perspective. If I took time to expose every intricate part of my life, it would take more than just this one book. But the honest truth is, I didn't write this book to tell my life story. I didn't write this book to show people my stars or my scars. I didn't write this book to receive acknowledgment or judgment. I didn't write this book to edify the articulation of my speech either. And I sure didn't write this with any intentionality of it being a best seller. I simply wrote this book to render why God takes pleasure in our brokenness, to expose how and why we hide from God and the world, the very thing we are intended to be: broken. Feel free to thank Adam and Eve for that part. I wrote this book to speak for broken people everywhere that are looking to be set free. I wrote this because I'm tired of our brokenness having to hide in darkness. I wrote this because I wanted to expose the power that lies in our brokenness. In our broken pieces, we find the perfection of God's justice, mercy, and love for our lives. God's perfection is made out of our imperfections. Once we begin to understand the pattern to our pain, we'll begin to realize that our traumas are for our gain.

My observation in life is that pain is the intentionality of our maturity. Pain is often the beginning stage of our traumas. But in parallel, it's also the planting seeds to our purpose. In our society, we have a natural tendency to avoid pain or get out of pain as soon as we come under it and rightly so. Who wants to experience pain? Who wants to sit in the pain? I don't. And I'm sure others don't either. But the reality is that pain doesn't come in our lives as a means to render us crippled but rather to unveil God's character. Psalm 119:71 says, "It was good for me to be afflicted so that I might learn your decrees." Pain teaches us about our capacity and the limits of our own innate abilities while showing us the unlimitable nature of God's power. Pain means to humble us and direct us back to God. But often we run to our own gifts and talents to deal with them or outside conveniences to soften the blow of our afflictions. Sometimes we experience pain just so God can show up and be the Father we never realized we needed.

177

I experienced a lot of pain throughout my life. And often I took to my career, the gym, or even nightclubs to avoid it. But those roads only led me to more broken pieces. I believe pain does two things: break us or mold us. What determines either direction is our willingness to yield and surrender to that pain. What do I mean? How do we surrender to pain? Why would we yield to it? I'm not saying to allow people to hurt us or walk all over us. That's not the spirit of my text. I'm simply communicating that pain, trauma, suffering are all things we will experience in our lives, whether we can control it or not. The point to surrendering and yielding is to appeal to God's character and understanding of why he'll allow us to endure such hardship. It's often in our pain, God wants to speak to us about our promise. Why? Because pain and hardships are almost always the only times when we feel incapacitated from life. It's the only time we stop all the running around. It's when we sit in silence and in our thoughts, trying to comprehend the measure of our pain. It's in those quiet and still moments of our affliction, I believe, that God wants to reveal his nature and his all-encompassing love for our life. Sometimes pain is momentary stillness that allows us to hear and see God's realness. That's why it tells us in Psalm 46:10, "Be still, and know that I am God."

God is always trying to get our attention. And often we can't hear it or see it because we are so occupied with the busyness of our own lifestyles. We don't realize he has something for us. But when trauma or pain hits, it often paralyzes us but not God. In those moments, God will often use our pain to reveal his promise for our life. So we need stop running from it. Take my advice, it's not worth it, it'll only lead down a track similar or worse than mine. God has something much better for us. We must allow God to speak to our heart through our pain. It's often always for our gain.

It took years for me to figure this out, because though I went through all those seasons throughout my life, God never changed. God is the same yesterday, today, and tomorrow. "For our light and momentary troubles are achieving for us an eternal glory that far outweighs them all." I surrender and yield to my light and momentary pain because what God has for me, I now know, is far better for what

I make my pain out to be. Be still, enjoy the process. we're in good hands.

Process

I used to think of my life by that one quote that says, "Whoever said progress was a slow process wasn't talking about me." It's very true to some degree, life itself is fast. It comes and goes. We are here only but for a moment. The progression of life is a very quick process—very true. But the process to purpose is anything but a quick process.

We live today in a society where we get things instantaneously: notifications, emails, messages, food, entertainment, and the list goes on. We live in an "I have to have it now" culture, and we're only precipitating this practicality more and more each day. And because we want life this way, we tend to think this way about ourselves as well. We want to make money faster, climb the ladder to success quicker, jump in and out of relationships in a haste, everything at all times in a rush to make our lives better for ourselves. We want it all, and we want it now. But what about the process, does it not matter anymore?

I used to be this way, I wanted to make a lot of money. I wanted quick recognition and validation. I wanted fast success and quick results in the gym and in my career. And through it all, I never paid much attention to the intricate wisdom that gets lost in the expedient nature of the process. I've come to understand that process is access to insight. I believe Jesus warns us about this in Luke when he says, "For what is a man profited if he gains the whole world and loses or forfeits himself." That text forces us to ask ourselves a very important question: Do we care more about who we become or who we are? In the middle of those two distinctions I believe is where process lives.

Tough, huh. It's because we live in a society and culture that emphasizes more about who we become rather than who we are. It's why we're constantly chasing an ever-changing wind and never satisfied. God doesn't care with who we become, he's already called that, which he predestined. God is more concerned about who we are—our heart. He warns us about this very thing in Jeremiah 17:9: "The heart is deceitful above all things and beyond cure. Who can understand it? I the Lord search the heart and examine the mind." God will take care of who we become, but he's more concerned about who we are.

The process of who we are needs to become more important than the process of who we become. This is exactly where I found myself. I had money, muscles, women, and plenty more. But on the inside, I was completely dead. I was focused on the wrong process. And because of that, I got off track of my promise. I wanted and needed to find the unfading beauty that Peter referred to in this text: "Your beauty should not come from the outward adornment, such as elaborate hairstyles and the wearing of gold jewelry or fine clothes. Rather it should be that of your inner self, the unfading beauty of a gentle and quiet spirit, which is of great worth in God's sight." But I realized that even to get there wasn't an easy or quick process.

To break free of my brokenness, I had to make myself available to God's process—meaning that I had to let go of those things I once valued. I had to let go and let God, no longer having control of the process but instead trusting God through the process. And that's hard because we're raised, taught, and validated in our society on the complete opposite. This is the wisdom we find in the process. When we are willing to submit ourselves to God, he'll make our paths straight. No matter the process of life we choose to take, we must recognize that it is a process in itself. But when we can slowdown from all of life's many distractions, it's when we'll recognize God's wisdom and revelation in the middle of it.

Our broken pieces are nothing more than flawed clay that God the Potter works out on his lathe to shape us in his perfection. That's the process we must all seek. Despite our stories, God wants to use our broken clay pieces to shape and direct us to our inherited destinies. Don't forsake the process because of the lack of progress, it's no doubt slow and sometimes hard to go through. But our reassurance is in the hands of the Potter, our Father. God is with us in the process, so it's time we change our perspective.

Perspective

While understanding pain and process is important, it means nothing without us changing our perspectives. This was one of the biggest changes I had to do. My perspective was broken in all three areas of my life: emotionally in how I saw myself and my story, mentally in how I viewed the world and people around me, and spiritually in how I understood the power of God and the message of Christ.

On my list of top ten areas of importance to me today, having a Godly perspective is at the top. I wasn't taught a lot about perspective growing up. I don't even believe I heard the word even uttered much in my presence. But as I've gotten older in life, I've realized its significant staying power and its contribution toward stepping out of my past and stepping into my purpose. I honestly think we live in a society where we teach more about success than we do about perspective. The reason I say that is because perspective is dimensional in nature, whereas success is fixed by a formed or intended outcome. Let me explain. Success speaks to "aim" and "resolve," while perspective speaks to "capacity" and "attitude." Not following?

Indulge me for a minute while I break down the famous Thomas Edison quote as an example. Thomas Edison, which I'm sure we all know was a great inventor between the 1800s and 1900s. Thomas Edison invented items such as the Dictaphone, autographic printer, kinetoscope, and the most notable invention was the incandescent light bulb. While inventing the light bulb, it was admitted that Edison failed numerous times throughout the process. And when this had been suggested, Edison's response back, which is one of the most famous quotes today, was "I have not failed. I've just found ten thousand ways that won't work."

Now in the context of success, Edison's "aim" and "resolve" was to create the light bulb, which as we see, Edison failed voluminously. With regard to perspective, Edison's "capacity" and "attitude" found success despite failure and found it in three dimensions from what I can see. First, Edison amassed a great deal of new data and insights. Without failure, Edison wouldn't have had insight. Sometimes the failures we experience is the sharpening of the keys to get us through the next door. In these failures, Edison's capacity for deeper knowledge, understanding, and perseverance expanded.

Second, Edison never allowed results to define purpose. Most any of us would have stopped at about the first one hundred tries. Shoot, maybe the first ten to twenty tries, we may have called it quits. But Edison didn't. Thomas Edison's attitude believed that failure was success. Catch that? That was a gem, grab it. This is the power of perspective. Edison understood that the process and wisdom obtained to get to success or an end result was equal, if not more important, to success itself. Lastly, Edison's confidence far exceeded the inabilities in the moment. Even though every result called Edison a failure, it also told Edison that success was around the corner. Failure is often the cornerstone of new direction. Edison's self-belief never wavered. Sometimes who we are has to be bigger than what the moment tells us we are. If there is anything to take away from this, it is that success is not certain—not at all. But the perspective we have toward life and the outcomes of life can be if centered on the right values.

Once I reestablished myself around Godly values, I was able to take on a Godlier perspective toward life. This was the problem with me. My values were limited by what society, corporations, and life had labeled *success* as instead of what God labeled as purpose. It warns us in Romans 12:2: "And do not be conformed to this world, but be transformed by the renewing of your mind so that you may prove what the will of God is that which is good and acceptable and perfect." I had spent most of my life conformed by the world. I talked like the world, dressed and walked like the world, thought and spoke like the world, and nearly lost my soul in the process. Instead I wanted to be transformed. I wanted a renewing of the mind. I was ready to pursue God's will to unlock my purpose. But in order to do so, I had to transform my perspective.

Today I do as it says in Colossians 3:2: "Set your mind on the things above, not on the things that are on earth." With this perspective every day, it allows me to break free in all three levels. Emotionally I see myself as God intended me to be and see my story, not with shame but as a gift, as a testimony to share with people so others themselves can have a breakthrough. Mentally I understand that life comes with suffering and pain, and that transformation is a slow process. But I can trust in God "being confident of this that he who began a good work in you will carry it on to completion until the day of Christ Jesus." And spiritually I've realized that God was always in my story, and now my new perspective allows me to align my life with God's power.

Power

I often and for a long time lived under the reality that the source of my power came from the strength of my resolve, my persona, my nature, my character. So I carried myself in a manner that seemed untouchable and very unapproachable. I didn't show an ounce of weakness, not one accord. My very presence evoked a dominance of someone not to be played with or taken lightly. It was the source of my strength.

It worked for me in two ways: to keep people from hurting me and to keep people from seeing me. That was how I yielded my power. That was what I thought masculinity was in my eyes. That was the power of a man I portrayed to the world because I assumed it's what I needed to be to get to where I needed to go. Man, was I wrong. Boy, was I broken. All that did was create the monster I became and the broken pieces I never realized I was hiding from. I was trying to be my own god in a way, not realizing I was destroying the very life God had graciously given me. Once I came to the space of confronting the man in the mirror and recognizing all the broken parts in my life, I realized that what I thought was power was nothing more than fictitious and calloused behavior because I was too afraid to be seen as weak. I needed people to see that I had it altogether even though I wasn't. I needed people to see that I was unfazed by obstacles even though I was broken. I needed people to see that I was happy even though I was miserable. I needed people to see I was strong even though I was weak. My brokenness led to my weakness, which opened the door to God's faithfulness. Paul articulates this perfectly in Corinthians when he says: "But he said to me, 'My grace is sufficient for you, for my power is made perfect in weakness.' Therefore I will boast all the more gladly about my weaknesses, so that Christ's power may rest on me. That is why for Christ's sake, I delight in weaknesses, in insults, in hardships, in persecutions, in difficulties. For when I am weak, then I am strong" (2 Corinthians 12:9–10).

This is when it clicked for me. This is when I realized the power of my broken pieces. This is why I decided to write my story, not to glorify my past but to show all my flaws, my hardships, my difficulties, my failures, and all my weaknesses, because through it, I was made strong. My weaknesses and God's perfections is the essence of this book. Now my power doesn't come from my gifts or my own doing but simply about God's faithfulness toward me and my obedience for him. The power of this text comes by process of the Potter's restoration of my broken pieces that was made perfect through my pain that started my life at a young age, which allowed God to lead me directly to my purpose. Now tell me, how good is that? That's what God is looking to do for each of our broken pieces. For as Paul said, "My grace is sufficient for you." So no matter how bad our story is or how ugly our broken pieces may look, God's power is sufficient for all. It's in God's power we are made and directed toward our purpose, but it's important to not miss the pattern.

Pattern

At first glance of reading this book, it looks like a lot of disjointed broken pieces connected by experiences. While that is somewhat true, we must go deeper to see the sensuality of the pattern. I must admit, when I first began looking back over my life, I as well just saw them as a bunch of individual broken pieces. But as I was lying in bed late one night, I heard God say to me, "Do you see the pattern?" For weeks, I wrestled with understanding this question, looking over my life many times over trying to see the pattern of what God was asking me. "What pattern?" I ask many times. Several weeks later, after wrestling with God and this question, the answer hit me like a flood of water. These broken pieces that had been spread over the course of my life began to paint a masterpiece of what God had been doing in the background of my life for over those thirty-four years.

Throughout the Bible, God shows us time and time again the importance he places in details, timing, order, and patterns. We see it first in creation when God created the heavens and the earth. We see it again when God had Noah build the ark, again when God instructed Moses on how to build the tabernacle, even later on when God had Solomon build the temple. All throughout the Bible, God shows us the patterns of his majesty and power, not just in structure but also in the hearts of people. This happened when Jacob wrestled with God for a blessing, and his name became Israel after his hip was disjointed, again when the angel of the Lord appeared to Gideon and called him a mighty warrior while he was threshing wheat. Even when God met Saul on the road to Damascus, his name was later changed to Paul after he had been known for killing believers. We also see it in the book of Ruth and Esther even though God is not mentioned one time throughout the pages, God is still masterfully at work in the background, stitching together the narrative of his perfect plan. There was an order, timeliness, and pattern to the lives of these mighty people of God that they had to go through to get to who God had called them to be. It's rarely ever a straight line to fulfilling Godly purpose. Often there is a pattern we all must go through to get out of us what power and purpose God has placed in us. Paul actually tells us this in Romans 8:29–30: "For those God foreknew, he also predestined to be conformed to the image of his Son that he might be the firstborn among many brothers and sisters. And those he predestined, he also called; those he called, he also justified; those he justified, he also glorified." The configuration of my life started long before the trauma. My trauma simply activated my pattern. "Before I formed you in the womb, I knew you. Before you were born, I set you apart."

Kintsugi is the Japanese art of putting broken pottery pieces back together with gold, built on the idea that in embracing flaws and imperfections, you can create an even stronger, more beautiful pieces of art. Gold refined in fire through Christ is what sealed the cracks of my brokenness. It tells us in Revelations 3:18: "I counsel you to buy from me gold refined in the fire so you can become rich and white clothes to wear so you can cover your shameful nakedness and salve to put on your eyes so you can see." The abandonment, unforgiveness, and identity were the broken pieces of the masterpiece.

My abandonment expanded into further cracks. It brought on the broken pieces of my issues with anger, pride, and vulnerability. My unforgiveness rendered its own broken pieces as well. It brought my shame, regret, and values. While my identity formed its own cracks in my life, it brought on my broken persona, self-esteem, and self-worth. The trauma brought about my pain. Searching for validation became the process I used to treat my agony, which allowed me to lose my perspective, becoming lost in a wilderness and destroying relationships along the way.

The two remaining broken pieces is what ties my pattern of brokenness altogether: fear and faith. I start the beginning of this book by saying, "I was raised in trauma." While that is true, it's the fear that was brought on as a result of my trauma that started my pattern. Fear was the very root of my brokenness. The fear allowed the cascading of all my broken pieces to come about. Trauma created the fear inside of my heart. Fear is what hit my life at a young age. It was the fear that created the first break in my heart. Fear is what allowed all the pieces of my life to spread the cracks through my heart. But fear didn't just create my brokenness, it's also what restored my heart.

The conversion of my faith and the pattern of my brokenness began and ended in fear. The fear that started my life was different than the fear that concluded the architecture of the masterpiece— meaning psychological fear versus Godly fear. Psychological fear is what I was raised in, Godly fear is what I was transformed in. Psychological fear is based on emotions of sensing danger or preparing for it. Godly fear is about respect and submission. This is what allowed for my renewed faith in God. This is what happens when a heart is refined by gold through fire. This is why my masterpiece is my brokenness. "He heals the brokenhearted and binds up their wounds" (Psalms 147:3). In that, I was able to find power through change and hope for my purpose. This was my pattern. The patterns of our brokenness aren't about staying broken, it's about God birthing and exposing purpose. It's about revealing the pattern to our story, the pattern of my testimony, the pattern and purpose of my ministry in Christ. "Come and hear, all you who fear God, and I will declare what he has done for my soul" (Psalm 66:16). It was in the pattern I was made whole.

Purpose

I never understood the significance of having a purpose until I found myself living without one. I find myself now asking, "How did I live so long without it?" When is the last time we've asked ourselves that question? What is my purpose? Have we ever considered why we're waking up each day? Outside of our career, family, relationships, outlets, and others activities, do we know what the purpose of our life amounts to? If we were to die today, would we have fulfilled it?

It's a deep question, I know, not one that can be simply answered easily. It took me years to find out mine. And even today, it's still being cultivated and polished. Purpose is defined by "the reason for which anything that is done, created, or exists, a fixed design, outcome, or idea that is the object of an action or other effort." This is what we were created for: purpose. God has a purpose for each and every one of us. "The purposes of a person's heart are deep waters, but one who has insight draws them out" (Proverbs 20:5). God has placed his purpose in the hearts of each of us. It's up to us whether we discover it or absolutely ignore it. That is the grace God gives to us.

I had to discover that my broken pieces, though a mess it was, had great purpose and meaning. Often people will give up on life, even commit suicide simply because of lacking purpose, seeing no reason to live any longer. I know what that window looks like. I battled that decision many of nights as I looked at all that my life had been through. But in the darkest of days, I saw that I was still here. I was still alive. I had made it another day. That reality told me that I was still here for something, that God hadn't deserted me or given up on me. At that point, I knew I had to fight for my purpose or die in my hopelessness.

So, how did I see purpose in the midst of my broken pieces? That's a good question. The answer is I didn't. I couldn't. All I saw was everything I ever knew and everything I ever did. There was no secret revelation or a voice calling me from the mountain. There was no burning bush or a visit from an angel. There wasn't a prophesy spoken over me or a vision given to me. I found my purpose simply by giving up on my predispositions. I had to let go of who I was trying to be, who society wanted me to be, who I thought I needed to be, and everything I wanted to be simply so I could find what I was purposed to be. There are many distractions on the road to purpose. But there is only one purpose, and it's in us already. "Whoever finds their life will lose it, and whoever loses their life for my sake will find it." Simply, I begin to find my purpose when I accepted and was willing to give up on my life. I've come to the reality that life is less about finding purpose in what we do. Rather it's about finding purpose in who we are.

We just have to ask ourselves if we're ready to give up on all the other proclivities we've allowed in our life. I'm convinced that purpose requires two things from us: sacrifice and obedience—two things that we don't practice or teach a lot in our culture today. It's why so many people around the globe struggle with depression, thoughts of suicide, hopelessness, and more, because unfortunately people live in the gap between a world who tells us we're not enough and our flesh that is covered in the reality of our own inadequacies. In between that gap is the broken pieces of our souls that are crying out for purpose.

For purpose, we must sacrifice our suggestive realities and fears and become obedient to God's wisdom and love. Sacrifice doesn't come without pain because it demands us to give up on what we value. And obedience asks that we do this every day. In doing this, we begin to throw down our selfish desires that are momentary anyways to take on the everlasting and enduring purposes of God. There are many broken people living without purpose today using the job, family, kids, or activities to derive meaning for themselves. But deep down, people will never be fulfilled or sustained without purpose. This is what God wants to give us today. He tells us in Jeremiah 29:11: "'For I know the plans I have for you,' declares the Lord, 'plans to prosper you and not to harm you, plans to give you hope and a future.'" All God asks of us is sacrifice and obedience. He'll workout the purpose despites our pieces.

The Broken Pieces

God can take broken pieces and turn them into masterpieces.

—Unknown

What are we doing with our broken pieces? Have we found our pattern? Are we going to choose to continue to live in them or ignore them and act like they don't exist? Go ahead. I only write this for people's consideration and to let people know that they're not alone. Today I don't claim to be perfect. In fact I'll always have cracks in between the places where God molded my clay together and transformed me. The cracks are left in the clay pot as a humble reminder of God's mercy, grace, and love, a reminder of who I used to be and how God saved me. The grooves in my clay pot are what tell this story today. It's the testimony of my life that everyone will see when they see me. The cracks in the pot tell everyone that though I'm saved and sanctified, I'm still flawed just like everyone else. The cracks in the pot demonstrate how "God can take our broken pieces and form masterpieces." I'm whole simply because Christ died for me, because he believed I was worth it.

I don't need people to think that I've done this walk all alone, because that isn't the case. God restored me when he could have discarded me. Today I tell this story to encourage others toward purpose, expose our broken pieces, and introduce us to a God that knows how to put us back together. I simply want to tell people that they matter, and I know this now because I had to realize I mattered even when I was broken. I came to the finite conclusion that I was broken in all the right places. If not me, then who else? God gave me purpose that set me apart from everyone else as did he do for you. Don't disregard it or ignore it because of the momentary things of this world or because you think you're too broken of an individual. You're no different than me. You as well are broken in all the right places. Are you ready and willing to allow God to mold you back to his purpose?

If you're here today alive and breathing, it's because you made it past your yesterdays. Despite the pain, affliction, shame, scars, disappointments, regrets, inadequacies, despair, insecurities, failures, and all the suffering endured, we've made it. Despite what our family, friends, employers, coworkers, community, neighbors, social media, or even what our haters have said about us, we've made it. Despite the journey we took, the path we chose, the decisions we've made, and the time it took, we've made it. We made it to today. We made it to this book. We made it. You'll be okay. I know that because I made it.

> On the day you were born, your cord was not cut nor were you washed with water to make you clean nor were you rubbed with salt or wrapped in cloth. No one looked on you with pity or had compassion enough to do any of these things for you. Rather you were thrown out into the open field. For on the day you were born, you were despised. Then I passed by and saw you kicking about in your blood. And as you lay there in your blood, I said to you, Live! (Ezekiel 16:3–6)

As for my broken pieces, my abandonment, unforgiveness, identity, values, self-esteem, self-worth, anger, shame, regret, persona, pride, vulnerability, fear, and faith, I finally found them. God always saw them. It was never about removing them. It was about acknowledging they exist and giving them to God, giving myself to God, allowing God to cut my cord, to wash me, to salt me, to cover me, a God who had compassion and took pity on me to bring me out of the wilderness. God saw me in all my brokenness, kicking and hearing the screams of my soul as I laid there in my blood and simply said to me, "Live," Today I live. Cracked and all, I live. Despite my past, I live. It's time we live. Are you ready to share your broken pieces?

ABOUT THE AUTHOR

William McGee stepped into this world on March 19, 1985 in Seattle, Washington, raised by two loving and nurturing parents. They were a small middle-class family. He was the second in line after his older brother. Few years later, his younger sister would be born. All of them where athletes growing up. Both his siblings play soccer while he stuck with football.

Growing up, he was a quiet and reserved kid, mostly kept to himself and didn't talk a lot but saw everything. What he saw and experienced throughout his life would be a catalyst for the man he ultimately became and had to overcome later on in life.

Today he is thankful to say that God delivered him from the former. While he had great success in his personal and career life, he believes ultimate success lies in the lasting legacy we leave for others to follow. And that's the path he's on today. These days he enjoys the simple things in life, intimate conversations, long walks, the smell of fresh flowers, reading a good book, or listening to a good message, spending time with family and love ones. He's thankful to live a life that started out broken all so that he could be made whole in all the right places.